THE BUDDHA IN THE ROBOT

THE BUDDHA
IN THE ROBOT

by Masahiro Mori
translated by Charles S. Terry

KOSEI PUBLISHING CO. • *Tokyo*

This book was originally published as two volumes, *Mori Masahiro no Bukkyō Nyūmon* and *Shingen*.

Edited by Ralph Friedrich. Cover design and layout of illustrations by Nobu Miyazaki. The text of this book is set in monotype Perpetua with handset Cloister Light for display.

First English Edition, 1981
Sixth printing, 1999

Published by Kōsei Publishing Co., Kōsei Building, 2–7–1 Wada, Suginami-ku, Tokyo 166-8535. Copyright © 1974,1976,1980 by Kōsei Publishing Co.; all rights reserved. Printed in Japan.
LCC 82–190923   ISBN 4-333-01002-0

Contents

Preface

Wheeled vehicles, whether they have two, four, or more wheels, are designed in such a way that they do not work properly unless all the wheels are rotating smoothly. If one wheel of your automobile lacks grease and is dragging behind the other wheels, you cannot make the car go straight just by steering straight in the ordinary fashion. The slow wheel pulls the whole vehicle in one direction or the other. A four-wheeled car with one bad wheel does not work as well as a three-wheeled car whose wheels are all moving properly.

The human brain might be likened to a very complicated vehicle with, say, a thousand wheels. On the same scale, the brain of a typical wild animal could be regarded as a four-wheeled affair, requiring only a minimum of lubrication. Though the animal's mental equipment is limited, the balancing and modulation of the parts is so simple that the animal as a whole operates efficiently, even gracefully. By contrast, keeping the thousand wheels of a human being's brain properly lubricated is so difficult that a fair number of wheels are apt to be operating badly at any given time. Unfortunately, we often fail to notice this until the pull of the malfunctioning wheels has thrown the whole mechanism out of whack and led it off in some completely unintended direction. Meantime, we fail to notice that somewhere along the way we have gone astray. This is the cause of the inconsistencies that prevent modern civilization from working properly.

What I have to say is really very simple. As human beings, we need to sit down and face the fact that not all of the billions of brain cells we are endowed with are functioning right. Our task is to try to make them work better. To do so is what I regard as religious conduct—the presence of those thousand wheels is what makes religion necessary for human beings where animals can get along without it.

Buddhism has a word for the condition in which our thousand wheels are in a state of ill repair and are functioning in jerks and bounds. The word is ignorance, which is seen in Buddhist philosophy as the fundamental cause of all evil. The diligent practice of religion, from the Buddhist standpoint, consists of searching out the malfunctioning brain wheels and oiling them so that they work the way they were intended to.

Once you have practiced religion to the extent of oiling and polishing each of those thousand wheels, your brain will work more actively than you ever thought possible. Things you never saw before will become as clear as day. The thousand-wheel vehicle will respond perfectly to your power steering, and you will be able for the first time to make it run exactly as you want it to. Soon you will find that your relations with other people and with the world around you are better.

If all human beings were running on all thousand wheels, the possibilities for the future would be infinite. The wisdom that we would have then would be what is spoken of in Buddhism as *prajñā*. We would have that unsurpassed enlightenment known as *anuttara-samyak-sambodhi*.

Even if all thousand wheels did not turn perfectly, even if only three or four of the bad ones began to operate smoothly, we would see things we have not seen heretofore. Our world view would be enlarged, and it would become that much easier to lubricate the still defective wheels. This in turn would lead us to an even broader view of things.

In this book I have written down some of the views that came to me years ago, when my thousand wheels began to turn as effectively as they are turning now, and when I was devoting much of my time to the study of robot engineering. A number of Buddhist specialists were of the opinion that my ideas agreed with Buddhist principles, and for this reason the essays were collected into a Japanese volume. Now an English version has been prepared.

In the year 1981 the world faces a great turning point. An enormous barrier rises directly before us. Whether we will be able bravely to make the turn, overcome the barrier, and arrive at the world of happiness and harmony on the other side is a question that concerns every single member of the human race. We can achieve this goal through Buddhism, which has withstood the criticisms of more than two thousand years and has proved itself to be the truest, the most perfect, the most universal, and the most magnanimous of religions. If this book succeeds as an introduction to the Buddhist way of thinking—which is to say to the universal principles of the universe—I shall be the happiest of authors.

In closing, I should like to express my gratitude to the translator, Charles S. Terry, and the editor, Ralph Friedrich.

THE BUDDHA IN THE ROBOT

I

What the Robot Taught Me:
Transparency and
Self-Enlightenment

It may surprise some of you when I say that I first began to acquire a knowledge of Buddhism through a study of robots, in which I am still engaged today. And it may surprise you even more when I add that I believe robots have the buddha-nature within them— that is, the potential for attaining buddhahood.

What connection, you may want to ask, can there possibly be between Buddhism and robots? How can a mechanical device partake of the buddha-nature? The questions are understandable, but I can only reply that anyone who doubts the relationship fails to comprehend either Buddhism or robots or both.

My own encounter with robots began, strangely enough, with a study I made of human fingers. This in itself was a venture into a scientific field not previously explored. How I came to be interested in fingers has to do with the fact that as a youth, long before I became a university professor, I was not what the ordinary person would regard as a brilliant student. The sad truth is that I entered high school at the bottom of my class and rose by the time of graduation only to second from bottom. That I am employed as a pedagogue now just goes to illustrate how unpredictable life is, and how difficult it is to see in advance what may result from a given set of circumstances.

I was born in a place called Nagashima—a village in Mie Prefecture lying in the delta created by the Kiso and Nagara rivers. My family moved to the city of Nagoya when I was two, however, and that is where I grew up. Despite my poor showing in high school, in primary school I had been at the top of my class. It was during the years at junior high school that my grades began to pursue a steady downhill course.

As you may well know, in Buddhist philosophy there is a distinction between ultimate causes for various phenomena and the immediate circumstances that bring them about at a particular time. In this instance, the ultimate cause for my scholastic downfall was that I was born with an inability to get interested in anything without going overboard. The immediate circumstance was that I happened to borrow a magazine called *Kodomo no Kagaku* (Science for Young People) from an older boy. An article in this journal left me with an uncontrollable fascination with radios.

At school, my grades in physics and mathematics remained fairly good, but I was terrible in English, terrible in my own native Japanese, terrible in history. Even so, because of my interest in radios and what makes them work, I made up my mind while still in junior high school that I would go on to higher schools and learn to be an electrical technician. This decision, I must say in retrospect, did more to make me happy in later life than the good marks I had made in primary school.

The school system in Japan was different then from now. The full course provided for six years of primary school, five years of junior high school, three years of high school, and three years of college. As a general rule, high school was intended as a preparation for people who intended to go on to the university, and going from junior high to high school was like going from high school to college today. The entrance examination was tough.

When I finished junior high, my mother was worried. "Do you suppose," she would ask, "that our radio nut can possibly pass the exam?" But I was perfectly calm. I would like to be able to say that this was because I was genuinely confident and brave, but the fact of the matter was that I was whistling in the dark. I am a born optimist.

My first choice of schools was the Nagoya Number Eight High School; my second, Nagoya Industrial High School, which is now Nagoya Institute of Technology. For a wonder, I passed the first examination at both schools.

"A regular whiz!" we all thought, but the rejoicing was premature. When the results of the second examination were posted, I found that I had flunked spectacularly at Number Eight and only a little less so at Nagoya Industrial High. I was moping about, wondering whether I should try for a third school, when a miraculous notice came from Number Eight High saying that I could enter as a substitute for someone who had dropped out. Then, as I was rushing to get ready to go, a similar telegram came from Nagoya Industrial High. With a feeling that must have resembled that of an acrobat who has executed a double flying somersault, I entered Number Eight High.

Only after I had finished the entrance procedure did I discover that the vacancy I was filling was not in the "A" science course, for which I had applied, but in the "B" science course. The "A" course led to engineering college; the "B" course, to medicine, agriculture, or biology. This was a blow, but I decided that I might as well go ahead. Somehow, I thought, I would manage to get from the "B" course into electrical engineering.

That, unfortunately, did not prevent the curriculum I was exposed to from being deadly dull. Instead of mathematics and physics, which I liked, I had to learn Latin names for all sorts of biological items. If you didn't know enough to call a nose bone an *os nasale,* you couldn't pass the exams.

"I'm an electrician," I kept thinking to myself. "Why do I have to go through all this foolishness?" I hated every minute I had to spend on subjects unrelated to electricity. In biology classes I often obscured myself in the back row of the tiered classroom and furtively read mathematics books while the teacher was lecturing about frogs and suchlike.

Possibly because of the unsanitary conditions prevailing in Japan in the early postwar period, in my third year I suddenly fell ill and had to go to the hospital. My ailment was diagnosed as scarlet fever, and I nearly died of it. Even after recovering, I had to be out of school for a whole semester and was unable to take any of the final exams. I had been due to graduate, but now it appeared as though I would have to spend another year as a third-year student. I rather liked the idea, because in those days students who failed and had to repeat a year had a certain prestige among their less experienced fellows. I could visualize myself basking in the glory of my new lease on youth. But then my teacher-supervisor called me in and said, "Mori, your average is only 52—second from the lowest—but we've decided to let you graduate."

The Second World War had ended the year before. Food was in such short supply that people went out shopping as though they were setting forth on a life-or-death mission. Almost everybody had his hands full just staying alive—hoarding what rice was to be found, treasuring sweet potatoes like gold. Students did not have the spiritual leeway to really put themselves into their studies. Officially, anyone who had an average of less than 60 at Number Eight High failed, but that year there were a hundred students who fell below that mark, and the passing grade was lowered to 50. This special dispensation enabled me to get by.

Taking off from the bottom, landing second from the bottom—I had hugged the ground in my flight through high school. Yet somehow I made it into Nagoya University.

There I finally realized my long-cherished wish to study electricity. They let me into the department of electronic engineering, and I wrote my graduation thesis three years later on the fairly recondite subject of solar electric waves.

But graduating from college did not put an end to my zigzag course. Japanese soldiers and civilians who had gone abroad had been repatriated in droves, and the country's material resources were virtually exhausted. It was a terrible time to try to find a job.

Word came to the university that one of the leading Japanese electric companies, Toshiba, was looking for people. I went to their offices in Kawasaki and took the employment examination.

In the subsequent interview, the personnel man said, "We want you to do some research on a new telephone receiver. You can start by studying bakelite as a possible material for it."

Feebly, I replied, "But the only thing I've really studied is electronics."

"In that case," he said tactfully, "perhaps the ideal thing for you to do is go on to graduate school."

In other words, no job at Toshiba.

Next, I tried taking the exam at NHK, the broadcasting network subsidized by the Japanese government. As it happened, NHK was not completely new to me. I played the flute a little, and while I was in college I sometimes worked as a part-time flutist for the NHK-affiliated symphony orchestra in Nagoya. The money came in handy for buying books on electronics, which tended to be expensive.

Luck would have it that the employment exam at NHK was held in the same room that the orchestra members had always used as a lounge when waiting to go on the air. I couldn't seem to settle down in it; somehow the memory of how we had laughed and talked there made me nervous. Whether that was the reason or not, I do not know, but I failed the test.

No job at NHK either.

The only thing left to do was stay at the university and continue my study of solar electric waves, and that is what I did. I also continued working as a pick-up flutist for the NHK orchestra. As it turned out, that brought about a great change in my life, for with the money I earned I bought Norbert Wiener's *Cybernetics,* a book that opened my eyes to a new world.

The science of cybernetics is concerned with the processes of control and communication in both human beings and machines. Wiener's book, the pioneer work in this new field of study, had created a sensation in the scientific world. My own encounter with it determined the future course of my life's work. Owing to its influence, I shifted from the study of solar waves to that of automated control. Presently I became a member of the Society of Automatic Control, Japan, and, through the good offices of its then sponsor, Professor Yasundo Takahashi of the University of Tokyo, entered that university's Institute of Industrial Science. In very short order, then, the electrician became a mechanic.

People in general seem to think that there isn't much difference between the study of electricity and the study of mechanics, but in fact they are worlds apart. If I had been allowed to enter the "A" course in high school and study electronics as I had wished to do, I am sure I wouldn't even have considered the possibility of changing fields in this fashion.

Until then, I had gone first in one direction and then another, to the extent that I was often disgusted with myself. It seemed to me at times that I must have an unconscious compulsion to lead a second-rate life. In the long run, however, everything fell in place. The seemingly desultory course of study I followed was, with respect to the work I eventually undertook, actually very efficient. After the change brought about by my introduction to *Cybernetics,* I felt that my life experience to date had been far more fortunate than that of the traditional bookworm who slaves in order to make high grades.

Let me make one point clear. My bad grades in school were not due to lack of study as such. I studied twice as much as most people, not because I had to, but because I was thoroughly absorbed. The only trouble was that what I was studying was not what the school was trying to teach me.

When I decided to become an expert on machinery, I realized that I would have to learn not only more about electricity but also about such things as gears, compressed air, and oil pressure, as well as the theory behind them. I began by attacking the field of automated controls, which meant, among other things, going to chemical plants and food-processing factories and actually operating various kinds of machinery. This experience convinced me that in order to devise better means of automation, it would be necessary to provide machines with hands and fingers.

The question was how to go about making them. Obviously, human hands and fingers would have to serve as the models. But did I know enough about the workings of human hands and fingers? Here, the obvious answer was no, and the only thing to do was to undertake a study of the subject, which I did. My collaborator was a fellow student named Tadashi Yamashita, now professor of control engineering at the Kyushu Institute of Technology.

Yamashita and I soon discovered that no one in the field of engineering—no one anywhere in the world—had ever made a study of how fingers work. Dr. Hakuzō Natori had published medical research articles on the special features of the human hand as a tool for labor and professional work, but we were able to discover nothing that dealt with fingers from the purely functional viewpoint.

"Good," I said to Yamashita. "You and I are the only two people in the world who are doing research in this field. We don't really have to read anything. All we have to do is look at our own fingers and see what they do. The materials for our research are all right there."

Once we started, we began to see what fantastic devices the human hand and fingers are. It was a revelation.

Have you ever stopped and considered the use you make of your hands and fingers in the course of a day's time? It begins early in the morning, because, if you are like most people, you cannot get out of bed without supporting yourself with your hands. When you are walking, your arms are needed to provide balance. You must use your fingers to brush your teeth, wash your face, wield your chopsticks or your knife and fork.

You can use your hands as a ladle to dip water. By opening your fingers slightly, you can convert this ladle into a sieve for sifting sand or pebbles. When you lift your hand to shade your eyes, it becomes a visor. When you point in a particular direction for someone, it becomes an instrument for communicating knowledge. When you test the water in your bath, it serves as a thermometer. When you count on your fingers, it is a type of calculator.

Consider also the arm that the hand is attached to. How well adjusted its length is to its functions! With it, you can reach any point on the surface of your body. If it were longer, it would get in your way. If it were shorter? Well, think of the unfortunate thalidomide babies whose arms extend only a short distance from their shoulders, and who are therefore unable even to pass things from one hand to the other. Those of us who are able to put our hands together in prayer ought to do so in reverent thanks for the ability.

Why do we have five fingers, no more, no less? And why are they different from each other in length and thickness? If you try making a robot that can hold a glass of water, you will begin to understand. The more precise your calculations, the more difficult the task seems. If the mechanical hand is strong enough to hold a glass without dropping it, it will probably crush it. If you make it too weak to crush the glass, it will probably drop it. But human fingers have the marvelous ability to sense the weight and strength of the glass and exercise just the amount of force needed.

Try watching people holding glasses of water. You will find that a majority of them do not use their little fingers. Does that mean that the little finger is superfluous? Not at all. When we put a glass down on a table without looking, as we often do, we unconsciously use the little finger as an antenna.

In Japan, clothiers these days often put a narrow pocket for a fountain pen next to the inside pocket of men's jackets. Not long ago, when I got on a train, I carelessly stuffed my ticket into my fountain-pen pocket, and when I tried to take it out later, I found I couldn't get at it. Red-faced, I stood at the exit gate trying desperately to extract the ticket, until I actually worked up a slight sweat. Finally, just as the ticket taker was ceasing to be able to contain his mirth, I discovered that my little finger was just the right size to go in and fish the ticket out. Saved by a small, thin digit!

It is no exaggeration to say that the human body couldn't function as it does if the little finger were not what it is and where it is. The lesson in this is that everything that exists has a role to play. There is a need in this world for tiny blades of grass, just as there is a need for tall massive trees.

The same is true of people. It is precisely because we all have different personalities and capabilities that we are able, when we try, to live together in harmony and to sustain each other effectively. This is the meaning of the parable of the herbs in the Lotus Sutra, which likens the Buddha to a dense cloud spreading over the earth and pouring down rain equally on "plants, trees, thickets, forests, and medicinal herbs, with their tiny roots, tiny stalks, tiny twigs, tiny leaves, their medium-sized roots, medium-sized stalks, medium-sized twigs, medium-sized leaves, their big roots, their big stalks, big twigs, and big leaves—every tree big or little, according to its superior, middle, or lower capacity, receiving its share."

This parable illustrates one of the great truths of Buddhism, which is the all-in-oneness and the one-in-allness of the buddha-nature. And I arrived at it merely by considering the little finger in relation to the other parts of the hand and body.

There is a Zen story about how Brahma once visited the Buddha, presented him a bouquet of flowers, and asked him to expound the Law. The Buddha silently responded by holding one of the flowers out for the people present to see. No one understood but the disciple Maha-Kashyapa, who reacted by smiling. The Buddha's meaning was that the Law of the Universe can be seen in a single blossom. It is thus self-evident and transparent for those who open their eyes to see. The Buddha rewarded Maha-Kashyapa by presenting him the "Eye of the True Law," which is nirvana.

Just as the meaning of the Law can be observed in a flower, it can be seen in your little finger. If you really get to know this digit, you will come to comprehend the entire human body and ultimately the world in which it exists. Know your hands, know your feet, know your torso, know your head—you will find that facts you never dreamed of appear before your eyes in rapid succession, as clear as light.

If you do not understand this, I must warn you that you will never be able to make a robot. Or, to put it conversely, any attempt you might make to produce a machine that functions like a human being must start with a knowledge of human beings.

As you work to produce an efficient robot, you begin to understand the feelings of a creating deity. "How shall I make the eyes?'' you ask yourself. "How shall I attach the ears?'' These questions force you to examine human eyes and ears more closely. You notice, perhaps, that a human being's eyes come equipped with lids, whereas ears do not. Why is this? Wouldn't it be better if we had "earlids," so that we could shut out talk we don't want to hear and protect ourselves from the noise pollution that surrounds us?

I once considered this question seriously and at some length. One morning, I tried putting stoppers in my ears while I was reading the newspaper. For a time this helped me concentrate, but all at once I saw a headline that caused me to do a double take: "Fire at Hot-Springs Hotel—Death Toll Still Unknown."

This started a fantasy. I see myself on a trip to a hot-springs hotel with some of the people I work with. After dinner, the others decide to play mah-jongg, but I don't know how to play, so I take a long bath in the hot springs and go to bed in the next room. The mah-jongg tiles go clickety-click, and I can't sleep. "How nice it would be," I think, "if I had earlids to keep out that racket." I roll up some paper tissues and plug them in my ears. This proving effective, I drop off into a deep sleep.

One of the mah-jongg players becomes so absorbed in the game that he drops a lighted cigarette on the tatami mat. Nobody notices it. After the game has ended and everybody has gone to bed, the mat begins to smolder and eventually a fire breaks out. The others wake up and flee for safety, but I continue to snore, ears immune to the sound of the confusion around me. . . .

Returning to real life, I practically threw down the newspaper, jumped to my feet, and removed my earplugs, still frightened by the vision of the flames closing in around me.

Each of a human being's senses performs an essential function, for which evolution has shaped it. Our eyes can see only what is in front of us, but our ears can catch sounds coming from before and behind, left and right, above and below. When a person is sleeping, ears detect the sound of approaching danger and cause the eyes to open. Something goes bump in the night, and the ears command, "Wake up." At that point the eyes take over and tell us whether the sound came from a burglar or a wandering tomcat. It was from my earplug experiment that I first learned an important fact about human ears, which is that they furnish us our earliest warning of danger.

We speak of analyzing things, which means fundamentally taking them apart in order to find out what makes them tick. In order to make a robot, we follow the opposite course and synthesize, attempting to put together a variety of parts in such a way as to create a machine that functions like a man. The process of discovering and selecting the parts is extremely educational. It brings to light many bits of basic knowledge previously taken for granted.

Why, I have asked myself, are there two holes in a human being's nose? Is it so that when a person catches cold one nostril can breathe while the other is stopped up? Why, for that matter, is the nose above, instead of below, the mouth? This question occurs to me because in a robot the nose could theoretically be anywhere. But as soon as I ask it, I see that there is at least one valid reason. Situated where it is, the nose can warn the mouth against spoiled food. The human body is designed in a very sensible fashion. The more I think of it, the more I marvel at its logic.

A man I know had an accident and lost one of his arms at the shoulder. He was soon provided with an artificial limb, which was a great help but which could not perform all the functions of the man's original arm—no mechanical device could, no matter how well designed. Yet the man soon discovered that the artificial arm gave him powers he had not previously had. Now, for instance, he could stick his hand into boiling water if necessary. In a rather curious way, when a part of the body that has been lost is replaced by artificial means, it invariably turns out that some new, and possibly unforeseen, ability or capacity has been added. In one sense, the artificial arm can be regarded as superhuman. It should be very convenient for washing dishes, for example.

This brings me to the subject of something that is of the utmost importance to human beings, namely, freedom of action.

Just what *is* freedom of action? Perhaps you will reply, "Freedom of action is the ability to do whatever you please, without restraint." But this answer is not enough. When you consider all

the infinite possibilities that exist in our universe, you see immediately that a human being, who has only two eyes, one mouth,
two arms, and two legs, is in many ways a very limited creature.
He has more capabilities than a dog or a cat, of course, but by
comparison with the all-powerful gods and buddhas, he is lacking
in both spiritual and physical powers, and consequently lacking in
freedom of action.

According to Professor Harumi Terada, who specializes in anat-
omy at Kitasato University, our ribs did not originate as a protec-
tion for our lungs. Millions and millions of years ago, when life
was confined to the sea, the ribs developed as a base for the mus-
cular twisting that propelled living creatures through the water.
In the early stages they resembled the bones of a present-day fish,
and it was only after a long process of evolution that they became
the casing that they are today. If you examine just one rib closely,
then, you see the limitations imposed by the whole history of
man's evolution.

It is possible to provide robots with five or six or any number
of eyes and arms. But what if this were true of people? A man with
a half dozen eyes and arms might be able to watch television,
read the newspaper, shave, and eat his breakfast all at once, thus
contriving to arrive at the office on time and avoid being scolded
by his boss. But if his eyes grew weak, how would the optome-
trist fit him with glasses?

The point is that, being built as we are, we suffer from certain
inherent restraints. There is no such thing as perfect freedom
of action in the objective sense. We do not exist entirely of ourselves and for ourselves. Yet we are not in the position of the robot, which exists entirely of and for others. If we understand the
limitations of our body, we can usually arrange to acquire greater
freedom. Once we have learned to accept the restraints that actually exist, without actually losing our volition and individuality,
we can consider ourselves free. This is another truth I learned
from studying the design of robots.

I mentioned earlier that as a student I sometimes played in an
orchestra. The orchestra, I think, illustrates the kind of freedom I
am talking about. The violinists, the cellists, the trumpeters, the

drummers are all under the control of the conductor's baton, but it is by accepting this control that they gain the freedom to express themselves musically—to do their thing, as it were. Far from losing themselves, they escape the chaos of disorganization and thereby acquire the opportunity to perform and be heard.

Through thoughts of this sort, I arrived at a very satisfying truth: We are bound within an organization known as society, but by being in harmony with others we can acquire maximum freedom.

No sooner had this idea come to me than I realized that this was what the Buddha was telling us twenty-five hundred years ago, when he spoke of the Transparency and Self-enlightenment of the Law. All things in the universe are related one to the other. The whole can be seen in any part. The universe is implicit in a little finger; its ultimate truth is embodied in a single flower. Freedom of action for the individual parts, including human beings, is attainable, but only by complying with the Law of the Buddha, which is self-enlightening.

2

What Is Me and What Isn't

One evening not long ago, a friend of mine asked me out for a sukiyaki dinner. He was obviously a little proud of the place he took me to, and I must say the food was superb.

As my chopsticks moved hungrily back and forth between bowl and mouth, a funny thought occurred to me. The meat I was consuming had come from a cow that I had never seen in my life, but now that cow was about to become a part of me. As I pondered this idea, my chopsticks stopped in midair, a slice of beef hanging from them.

"What's the matter?" asked my friend. "Something wrong with the meat?"

"Oh, no," I replied. "I was just wondering. At exactly what point does this beef become *me*? It's still not me when I put it in my mouth. It's mine, I suppose, but it isn't *me*. Does it become part of me after it passes down my esophagus into my stomach? Or does it still have a separate existence inside me?"

Unhesitatingly, my friend answered, "Very simple. The meat doesn't become you until it's absorbed by your stomach and converted into flesh and blood."

"I suppose you're right," I said, somewhat reluctantly, "but if that's true, what about air? I am sure that the air around me is not part of me, but does it become part of me after I breathe it into my lungs?"

"Well, shortly after that, at any rate," answered my friend, now a little less sure than before.

We tossed the question around for some time. What about the vegetables? Or the water we were drinking? When do they cease to be themselves and become part of us? The more you consider the matter, the more intricate it becomes.

The glass of water, for example. It appears to be absorbed inside us and become part of us. But later it comes out of us in the form of vapor and evaporates. From what point to what point can it be considered to be an integral part of our bodies? One scientist has told me that during a night's sleep a human being emits about a cup of water that is normally absorbed by pajamas or bedding. From experience I know that if I put on a vinyl raincoat and go out for a brisk walk the inside of the raincoat is soon dripping wet. This means that the water that had become part of me is no longer part of me.

When I breathe, I take in oxygen and give out carbon dioxide, which is a compound of oxygen and carbon and is therefore heavier than oxygen. The effect, then, is that I am exhaling more matter than I am inhaling and, in a strict sense, becoming slightly lighter with each breath I take. Can I consider the air I breathe to become part of me when in reality I am giving the atmosphere back more than I took from it?

I tell people that I weigh 60 kilograms, and I consider these 60 kilograms to be *me*. But I know that when I climb a flight or two of stairs my weight decreases by a gram or so. Whenever I exercise, I become lighter by an amount corresponding to the energy I have used. Is the weight I take on or lose a part of me, or is it not? The borderline between what is me and what isn't at any given time is difficult to draw.

As I consider questions of this sort, I am reminded of the Buddhist axiom that "nothing has an ego." This means that nothing in this universe exists in isolation; everything is linked with everything else. The implication of this fundamental Buddhist teaching is that unless we can annihilate our egos, we cannot see the world or the people in it as they really are.

Most people have little trouble understanding this truth from the intellectual viewpoint. Before our eyes we see a book or a desk or a fountain pen and realize that we are related to these objects because they permit us to read and write and study. When someone in our family is in trouble, we ourselves experience distress—there are blood ties that hold us together. But how can I, toiling away in the teeming city of Tokyo, have any true sense of relationship with a primitive tribesman living in the wilds of Africa? More important, how can anyone actually annihilate himself and become nought while still continuing to live?

One part of me knows that I exist. I can see with my own eyes that I have two arms and two legs just like everybody else. If somebody gives me a poke in the nose, I know I exist, because I can feel the pain. This seems to suggest that there is no way to do away with the ego, and that is the conclusion that most people reach.

But how does this square with the fact that it is difficult, if not impossible, to decide at any point just what is me and what is not? Is there some line of demarcation between the things that are related to my ego and the things that are not? Or is the human ego stranger and more complicated than it seems on first consideration? Perhaps the robot can help answer these questions.

When I start to make a robot, I have to gather materials: a motor or two, some aluminum sheet, steel bands, transistors, copper filaments, and so on. A robot is made by putting these components together according to one scheme or another, and if we are to understand the robot fully we must understand the parts. What are they? Where do they come from?

Let's start with the motors. Motors are made mostly of steel and copper. Where do we get the steel? From a foundry, of course. How does the foundry make the steel? Obviously, it cannot be manufactured from nothing. It must be produced from a material known as iron ore, or, to be more exact, from a chemical compound called iron oxide, which can be broken up into iron and oxygen.

Where does the iron ore come from? It is mined in the mountains of Australia, China, and Africa and brought to Japan in cargo vessels. Africa? Yes, Africa. Through the steel and the iron ore, the robot I am making is related to the home of the African tribesman I spoke of.

What happens when we substitute people for robots? What are people's bodies made of? In the final analysis, they are composed mostly of carbon or hydrogen atoms, as can be seen from the fact that when we die and are cremated most of us goes up the crematorium chimney in the form of carbon dioxide gas. Only the ashes are left. We are prone to think of the carbon dioxide gas as being our own, but it is obvious that we ourselves did not create it.

Carbon dioxide comes to us from the plants and vegetables that we consume every day. How do the plants and vegetables happen to have the necessary carbon? They receive it from the air. A substance called chlorophyll, which is present in their leaves, enables them to use the sun's energy to extract and absorb carbon from the carbon dioxide flying about in the air.

Where does the air come from? From Siberia, from Africa, from all over the world. The earth's atmosphere is constantly shifting from place to place. The carbon dioxide it contains might come from anywhere. And the carbon I receive from vegetables may, for all I know, have entered the air as smoke from the burning body of a lion caught in an African forest fire. Similarly, my eyeball may once have been part of a black man in Rhodesia; or it may have been a cluster of bacteria living in the sea. The carbon within what you call yourself may one day be part of a polar bear in Alaska or a kangaroo in Australia.

"All right," you may say, "but before we ever take nourishment from food, our bodies are created within the wombs of our mothers, aren't they?"

This is a reasonable question. When we are born into this world, we do seem to have been given a portion of our mothers' flesh. Yet when sperm fertilizes ovum and a baby is conceived, the most important element is not ordinary flesh, but the hereditary information contained in DNA, an acid found in chromosomes. The molecular structure of DNA determines our sex, our looks, and to a large extent our personalities.

Once these features are decided, as they are at the time of conception, it remains for our mothers to furnish us with flesh and bones. This they do by eating vegetables from the greengrocer's, beef and pork from the neighborhood butcher, bread from the baker. Any of these foods, supplied by a production and distribution system that may involve millions of people in many countries, could contain carbon from our Alaskan polar bear. How can you and I say then that *this* carbon is mine and *that* carbon is yours? At the atomic level, all carbon is the same; no two carbon atoms differ in the slightest, either in form or in character.

When you look at the problem this way, it begins to seem only natural that we have trouble distinguishing between what is us and what is not. Our chemical and physical composition is such that no one is entitled to say, "This body is mine, all mine." When you have mastered this point, you are ready to start thinking about "nothing has an ego."

Let me attack the same idea from another angle. Every schoolchild knows that there is something called the force of gravity that prevents us from flying off into space when we jump up in the air. Fewer people know, or remember, that the pull of our turning earth planet is only one instance of what scientists speak of as the universal law of gravity. According to this principle, every mass exercises a certain pull on every other mass. Everything on or in our planet—the house next door, the pebbles in the driveway, an automobile running along the highway a hundred kilometers away, great boulders buried thousands of meters below the ground, the water in the ocean, each and every human being—is trying to attract everything else to itself. And all these things are constantly being pulled toward the center of the earth. We are all linked by gravitational ties.

Furthermore, gravity extends throughout the universe. The sun and the earth tug at each other, and both have gravitational links with Mars, Venus, Saturn, Jupiter, and the other planets. Celestial bodies millions of light years away exert a force upon our solar system, as well as on all other solar systems.

In order to set an accurate standard for the measurement of time in Japan, the Tokyo Astronomical Observatory at the University of Tokyo maintains an atomic timepiece, moved not by springs and cogs but by the oscillations of atoms in a piece of cesium. This marvelous clock has been adjusted in such a way as to eliminate even the distortions that might be caused by the gravitational pull of the dozen-odd moons of Jupiter! Similar chronometers are in operation in many other countries.

Are you impressed with the extent of the links that bind everything together? Perhaps you will find it even more impressive that, although the existence of universal interrelations was not proved scientifically until the twentieth century, it is implicit in "nothing has an ego," the principle laid down by the Buddha 2,500 years ago.

The heart said to the kidney, "Don't be so uppity, Buster. Where would you be if I stopped sending you blood?"

The kidney retorted, "And where would you be if I stopped cleaning out the dirty blood you send?"

To many people lying in hospitals, the idea of the kidney and the heart failing to recognize their mutual interdependence would not be funny. When one outdoes the other, both are damaged, but the real victim is the body itself.

I doubt that anyone fails to recognize that the various mechanisms in his body are linked in a complicated network. A command from the brain goes out via the spinal cord and the nervous system, and the body moves in response. In an opposite fashion, impulses coming in from the ears or eyes or fingertips are gathered within the brain. The energy with which the brain's orders are carried out is transported throughout the body by blood vessels and capillaries.

The world is linked together in the same way, but somehow the connections seem constantly to be coming unhitched. The reason is that people draw superficial boundaries between bodies and then create distinctions between that which is within and that which is without. This is the basis for the concept of self or ego. The fact that a human being's body is physically separate from other bodies leads to the illusion that each body possesses a discrete existence.

When we complain that a person is always feeding his own ego, we mean that he is selfish. A particular form of selfishness is the notion that one is completely independent of others.

The opposite of selfishness is selflessness, which may be defined as acceptance of the truth that "nothing has an ego." Selflessness means realizing that there is no fixed barrier between yourself and what is around you; it means knowing that you are linked with every other form of existence, animate and inanimate. You have arrived at the plane of selflessness when you are able to think, "If this is me, then that is me too: the whole universe is me."

Our world is composed of innumerable atoms. Dense concentrations of atoms form bodies that we call John or Bill or desk or automobile or building. Thin concentrations are what we call air or space.

The Buddha, with his superior vision, recognized that, although the world is one, it is not a homogeneous blob, but an integrated network of phenomena linked together in an infinite variety of ways. All existence is selfless, but at the same time every thing and every being has an identity. The Buddha did not fail to see that in order for things to be linked they must be separate. This takes us into the realm of the philosophy of technology, rather than science, as I can demonstrate by reference to nothing more recondite than the glasses I am wearing.

To make a pair of glasses, it is necessary to cut a piece of glass in two, shape the pieces, and fit them into holders. The next step is to cut pieces of metal with which to make fittings that will link the holders above the bridge of the nose. It is not enough simply to snip out pieces; they must be fitted together in such a way as to ensure the functioning of the glasses. Each section therefore must be cut in a particular way.

Almost everything in the world is made by cutting things apart and then fitting the parts together. The clothes you wear, the houses you live in, the furniture inside the houses—all are made in this fashion.

Obviously, the manner of cutting is fundamental. No tailor, no matter how clever, could put together a decent suit from an assortment of random cuts from a bolt. No carpenter, no matter how skillful, could build a house from pieces of wood cut to no particular size or shape.

Of prime importance are the joints—the places where pieces are linked one with another. If the ends and edges do not fit together, the parts can be no more than useless bits of material. It is much the same within the society of human beings. If the borderlines along which they come in contact are not adjusted, people cannot live together.

Recently a new crop of freshmen entered the university where I work. Having cut the ties they formed in high school, they must now find new links in college. Four years from now, when they graduate, these links will be severed, and new ones will have to be formed at the companies where they find work. From these connections, new organizations and new work will be created.

The links at this later stage will reflect the particular skills and abilities that the graduates have acquired during their years at college. It is because they will have formed separate personality traits and become distinct one from another—in other words, because they have developed egos—that they can be cut apart from one group and linked to another.

Engineering begins with the science of cutting. In the field of personal relations, the point of departure for creating closer and more effective connections is to discover how to "cut out" one's own personality. I like to think of this as a combined process of separating and combining.

If you visit a factory where automobiles are manufactured, you will find an enormously long complex of machinery known as a conveyor system. This is an assembly line along which cars are put together as they move from one end to the other. If one part of the system goes bad, it cannot simply be removed; it must be replaced by a duplicate part that is not defective. Should a flaw in the assembly line go neglected or unnoticed, no end of damage can result.

The cultural crisis that faces the world today seems to me to be the result of faulty connections along the assembly line that has produced our material civilization. This is why I am fascinated with robots. I keep thinking I might discover through them how to correct the defective links.

The robots I would like to build would be machines that could be detached at will and relinked with other parts to function more efficiently. I would describe these as robots of a "separate type" in which the convenience of being independent is given priority. The advantages of a separate type are seen in a package of cigarettes, from which the individual pieces can be removed one by one. A more complicated example would be a deck of cards; it is precisely because the individual cards are of a separate type that a player can from time to time make a grand slam.

If human beings had hands like skier's mittens, with no divisions between fingers, I do not think modern civilization could have been created. Because our fingers are separate, they are able to perform a great variety of functions. More specifically, they are able to use a great variety of tools, not the least important of which are the pen and the typewriter.

Human beings are connected with all things, as are the fingers with the hand; at the same time, they have individualities, as do the separate fingers. We all belong to what I call the separate type. No two of us are exactly alike; we all have different faces, different natures, different capacities. And the very differences make it possible for us to join together and do great things.

How would it be if the world were composed of homogeneous lumps of matter? There would be no distinction between plants and animals, rivers and mountains, black and white. In this monotone existence, there would be an appearance of harmony, but in fact existence would be chaos.

Even if we limit ourselves to the world of human beings, wouldn't this be true? If everyone had the same brainpower, it would be impossible to link people together—there would be no need for it. It is because people have different faces, different bodies, and different capabilities that the possibility of linking them all together exists. Paradoxical though it may sound, then, we can only conclude that the creator, in his wisdom, made us distinct one from another in order to bring us together in perfect fusion.

Recently I visited a Zen temple and had a long talk with the priest. In the course of our conversation, I remarked, "The more I study robots, the less it seems possible to me that the spirit and the flesh are separate entities."

"They aren't," replied the priest.

I continued, "The idea that the body is some sort of container that the soul settles down in, only to move to different quarters after the body dies, seems to me unthinkable."

The priest gave me a Buddhist explanation. "To split the body from the spirit gives rise to what we call discrimination," he said. "Discrimination divides things into good or bad, useful or useless, and sets up hard-and-fast rules that enslave people. Buddhism abhors the idea of dividing things in two. Buddhism combines the spirit and the body into an entity."

This seems to me to fit in with my idea of separating and combining simultaneously. I might put it another way: the spirit and the body are carefully cut so that they can be effectively unified.

In recent years much attention has been focused on problems that beset contemporary civilization—problems such as pollution and the drying up of our natural resources. Everybody has become familiar with the science of ecology, which attempts to preserve our natural environment. I am struck by the emphasis ecologists place on natural flow, because it seems to me that this concept is also in agreement with my idea of separating and combining.

Ecologists have five basic principles: (1) that everything is in a state of change; (2) that all things are connected one with another; (3) that no wisdom exceeds that of nature; (4) that nothing exists without meaning; and (5) that there is fundamentally no such thing as waste matter. In sum, the idea is that the world grows and develops because all existence is in a state of interrelated flux. Anything that impedes the flow of nature is bound to cause trouble.

To hoard water, money, or knowledge for selfish purposes is to defy the principles of nature. The point in life is not to accumulate goods or information, but to find ways of making them flow more freely among a maximum number of human beings.

To make water flow, it is necessary to create a difference in height, for water will flow only from high places to low places. In human society, we can increase the flow of nature by maintaining a low posture.

When you go to a scholar or an expert and ask him to teach you, the best way to ensure a flow of information from him to you is for you to practice humility—put yourself on a lower level than your instructor, so that his knowledge can flow down more freely. If you attempt to be his equal—to stand on the same level—you are not likely to learn much. Still less will you learn from anyone whom you hold in contempt.

Yet, if I am right about separating and combining, if differences exist in order that we may all be linked together, then everyone you encounter has something to contribute to you. The way to receive it is to keep yourself in the proper respectful position.

3

Foreseeing Delayed Reactions

It seems that we human beings have a strong urge to force all things outside ourselves to do as we wish them to do. This statement is not intended as a broad philosophical principle; it is merely an observation I have made over a number of years. Ask yourself whether it is true in your own life. Review the things you do from day to day, and see if you are not constantly attempting in one way or another to impress your will on your surroundings. If you are normal—which is to say, if you are like me—you will see that you spend a great deal of your time and energy trying to control things.

Some things are easy to control: if you come home from work dead tired and want a hot bath, it is fairly easy to draw just enough water into the tub at just the right temperature. It is also simple to control your food intake—you eat until you are full and then stop eating. But there are many instances in which control is difficult because our attempts to assert our will do not have the foreseen results. Sometimes this is because we have ignored certain factors; sometimes it is because there are too many factors for the human brain to grasp all at the same time.

37

It used to be that nearly all Japanese trains were pulled by steam locomotives. Nowadays the railway system has been electrified and steam engines have become a rarity, whose billowing smoke and great chugging pistons and obsolete coal tenders seem to have a great attraction for the young. The steam locomotive operates on essentially the same principle as the whistling teakettle in your kitchen—water boiling in a container yields steam, which when forced into a closed chamber produces the pressure needed to turn wheels. Since the locomotive is using steam whenever it is running, the amount of hot water in the boiler gradually decreases. It is the job of a train crewman to feed new water in to replace that which has boiled off. All this sounds very simple, but in fact it is not so easy to restore the water level inside the boiler once it has dropped.

Picture yourself in the locomotive. You suddenly notice that the water level in the boiler has gone down. Instinctively you rush to add water to the tank, confident that the water level will rise. But to your astonishment, when you turn on the water valve, the water level gauge shows a drop rather than a rise. Apparently, more water from outside is yielding less water inside the tank.

Adding water to a boiler is not like adding it to a fish tank. If the boiler is in operation the addition of cold water will immediately bring about a lowering of the water level. The reason is not difficult to understand: when the water is boiling, that part of it which is about to boil off forms bubbles that raise the water level; when new water is introduced, the temperature drops below the boiling point and the bubbles disappear. After you have added a certain quantity of water, of course, the gauge begins to rise again. But if the initial drop in the level has caused you to panic and shut off the water supply, your engine may now be in danger of overheating and exploding.

So if you do not know the nature of boilers—or, to state it more generally, if you are ignorant of the situation you are trying to deal with—the steps you take to exercise control are apt to backfire. Maybe when it is all over and the reason for your blunder has been explained, you can laugh it off as a joke on yourself. But there are all too many cases in the world today when our attempts to control our surroundings have led to results that are anything but laughable.

Just after World War II, we had a severe shortage of rice in Japan, and the government began pressing farmers to produce all the rice they could. Today we have so much rice that we don't have enough warehouses to keep it in. Far from encouraging rice production, the government is giving the farmers "incentives" to cut back on their rice acreage. Yet even as this goes on, the media are warning us of an impending world food shortage. The moral of this story is that when we attack problems too precipitously, the results are likely to be a new crop of problems, more difficult than the original ones.

From time to time, economists warn that we are in for a big depression. Dutifully, we turn pale at the very thought. The government begins pumping money into the economy to right and left, and prices begin to soar beyond anybody's reach. Surprised at this result, the government's financial wizards hasten to adopt a high-interest retrenchment policy, which usually leads to a worse depression than the one foreseen at first.

Our lack of ability to predict the outcome of what we are doing is not limited to the spheres of politics and economics. How many parents have sacrificed to give their children the best of everything, only to find later that the children have grown up to be monsters! The story of the devoted mother or father who is later abandoned or forgotten by ungrateful offspring is one of the mainstays of the Japanese melodrama.

In the world we live in today, it is not easy to make things turn out the way we want them to. We all think we are aware of this, but I sometimes wonder if we realize the extent of our helplessness. We seem curiously unable to distinguish between that which we can control and that which we cannot.

Once I carried out a simple but interesting experiment with water tanks, starting with one and working up to four. In the first stage, there was a single tank with a hole at the bottom through which water could drain off. Above the tank was a spigot from which water could be added. The problem was to discover how to keep the water level in the tank constant. As it happens, any child can do this. It is necessary merely to see that the same amount of water comes in from the spigot as issues from the outlet.

The next step was to raise the level of the water 5 centimeters and then keep it constant. This is easy, too. You open the spigot enough to admit more water than is draining off at the bottom; then, when the level in the tank has risen 5 centimeters, you reduce the water from the spigot to the amount exiting from the drain. The only point of interest here is that it takes a little more water from the spigot to maintain the higher level than it did to maintain the original level. This is because the added depth increases the water pressure at the bottom and forces more water to drain off than before. The trick here is that in order to maintain the same level you must keep your eye on the water in the tank rather than on the stream flowing out at the bottom.

If the drain hole were closed, any amount of water added at the top would raise the water level proportionately. In Buddhist terminology, we could say that the *cause,* which is the water coming in from above, leads immediately to the *effect,* which is the rise of the water level in the tank. If the drain hole is open, the water level does not rise so rapidly as before, and we must conclude that the cause is producing a delayed effect. When the delay is no more than is involved here, a human being is able to cope with it simply by keeping his eye on the level of the water and adjusting the spigot accordingly.

To regulate the cause in accordance with the effect is an example of what scientists call feedback control. So long as feedback control can be carried out easily, we human beings have little difficulty making the things around us behave as we wish them to.

The experiment is continued with two water tanks rather than one. The water flows from the spigot into the first tank and then through a hole in its bottom into the second tank, which also has a drain hole at the bottom. Is it possible, by keeping your eye on the water level in the second tank and controlling the spigot accordingly, to maintain a fixed level in the second tank? As a matter of fact it is. Try it and see. It is not quite as easy as it sounds, but nevertheless possible.

Let us now increase the number of tanks to four. Can the water level in the bottom tank still be maintained in the same fashion as before? Your inclination will probably be to say yes, because the problem seems to involve the same principles as when two tanks are being used. And until about twenty years ago many scientists would have agreed with you. In fact, however, it is impossible for a human being without outside aid to adjust the water line in the fourth tank to a desired level. The reason is that the level of water in the fourth tank is now affected by factors too complicated for the human brain to deal with intuitively. The delay between cause and effect is too long for the human imagination to encompass.

In the arrangement of tanks I mentioned, if water is fed rapidly from the spigot, a fair amount of time must elapse before any effect at all can be seen in the fourth tank. As one would expect, the water level first rises in the first tank, then in the second, third, and fourth in order. But there comes into operation a complicated series of connections linking the water levels and the water pressures in the various tanks. The actual flow of water into the fourth tank cannot be calculated without recourse to more or less advanced mathematics. It can happen that the water level in the lowest tank reaches a minimum when the spigot is turned on full and a maximum when the spigot is turned off for a few seconds. The ordinary human being attempting to control the level in the lowest tank is apt to become annoyed or frustrated. He feels that the water is playing tricks on him.

If you have followed the explanation of the water-tank experiments, perhaps you are beginning to see the point I am driving at, which is that the world we live in is full of annoying things that do not react as we want and expect them to react. Most of us find this very frustrating, and nearly all of us are given to taking our frustrations out on others. We see this around us every day.

"The whole business is upside down," laments a white-collar worker. "I slave for this company and get nowhere, while these guys who know how to pull the right strings get promotion after promotion."

"What is the world coming to?" inquires the socially minded

scholar. "No matter how you look at it, everything just gets worse and worse."

People beat their breasts, shout their complaints, and air their bitterness, but, far from causing society to run more smoothly, they succeed only in creating an atmosphere of mutual recrimination and mistrust. Everybody blames everybody else for his difficulties.

What good does this do? Will it solve our problems? Wouldn't it be better to recognize that our difficulties are much deeper? At least as deep as the four-tank experiment, which is vexing because it appears soluble but isn't?

The structure of contemporary society is no four-tank matter. Perhaps a hundred tanks might rival it in complexity. The world is full of problems that only get worse when we attempt to solve them in a hurry. All too frequently we adopt methods that seem logical but in the end accomplish the exact opposite of what we intended.

The time has come to cool our heads and think some of our difficulties through to their fundamental causes. Ultimately, this is the only way to arrive at solutions that work.

Let us consider the pollution of our environment, for example. A number of irate conservationists argue that pollution is caused by business enterprises whose factories pour their waste chemicals into our rivers or belch sulfurous smoke into the sky. Others, equally irate, contend that the trouble is with machines, which were intended to serve man, but now more often than not exercise dominance over him.

There is no doubt that manufacturing enterprises have been a large source of pollutants. Yet it is a fact that the production carried on by these businesses is for the most part needed to support the expanded population of our times. We must try then not to eliminate industry but to discover just where it goes astray. What bad features does it have that lead to pollution? Who is responsible for these features? By isolating the causes of pollution and eliminating them, can't we save ourselves from environmental despoliation?

One difficulty, of course, is that when you get down to the task of examining a large company, it is very difficult to put your finger on the truth. If a man is walking down the street and another man suddenly assails him, it is clear that the second man is at fault. But in business enterprises it is often uncertain who is responsible for a mishap. Some will argue, with theoretical justification at least, that the company's president is to blame; admirers of the president will almost certainly counter that he is of much too high character to be suspected of seamy conduct. What about the board of directors? They too, it will be said, are far too honorable to inflict damage on innocent people knowingly.

Well, then, is the damage caused by machines after all? How could it be, when the machines are designed, bought, and operated by human beings? Arguments attempting to fix responsibility can go on indefinitely.

When the offending company is of the autocratic type, in which the boss's word counts for everything, it is possible that pollution may be brought under control by discharging the boss. Today, however, most company presidents are more than aware of the immense losses their firms may suffer if found guilty of spreading pollution. The department and section chiefs in charge of the actual work have as a rule taken all preventive measures they can think of to avoid pollution. When pollution occurs anyway, who is to be faulted? Even the ordinary employees of the company do not know; they only know there is nothing they can do about it. The fault lies with some invisible monster.

One problem that aggravates all our contemporary difficulties is the mammoth scale on which everything—government, business, the school system—operates. Size as such is of little importance; what matters is that numerous organizations have grown so large that it is difficult for them to respond promptly to the problems that arise. It seems to me that this tendency is observable throughout our social structure.

Suppose a man working in a factory recommends a change of procedures in his section. His memo goes to a "water tank" called the superintendent or foreman, who sends it to a "water tank" called the section chief, who forwards it to a division chief, and so on up to the president. The president takes a look and says, "That's a good idea. Let's do it." His decision is then conveyed back down the tiers of water tanks to the factory, where by this time the problem has most likely either disappeared or been solved by impromptu methods. In an age of giant organizations, we must face the fact that big wheels turn slowly.

This sort of thing annoys some people so much that they go to extremes in the opposite direction. Just a few weeks ago I received a post card from some graduates of our university, who had studied under me. "It has been five years since we left the university," the card said, "and we would like to organize a class reunion, which we hope you will attend." Since I always enjoy getting together with my old students, I replied that I would be delighted to come. As requested, I signified a date that would be convenient for me.

As a rule, when people send out an invitation of this sort, they wait at least two weeks for answers to come in before setting a final date, but the organizers of this party went ahead and reserved a banquet room in a hotel on a specific date before the replies had come in. As it turned out, almost no one was able to go on the appointed day, and the reunion had to be canceled.

Here is modern man for you. He says to himself, "If I do *this,* then *that* should happen." But somehow things go wrong and *that* does not happen. Annoyed and perplexed, he rushes into some other course of action, only to find that it works no better than the first, if as well. This is the way most people live today, and this is the way contemporary society functions.

Suppose the whole world came under the dominion of a powerful dictator and everybody was required to obey the rules so strictly that it would be possible not only to predict results but even to apply feedback control to the causes. Such a society might conceivably function efficiently in some ways, but it would provide happiness for no one.

Is it not possible to create a society in which people can for the most part do as they please while at the same time living in harmony with their neighbors? That, to my way of thinking, would be a genuinely human and humane society.

Recently I went swimming at a beach near Tokyo. As I was walking along by the waterline, I came upon a starfish that had become entangled in a fisherman's net and had then been discarded on the shore. Out of curiosity, I turned the creature over on its back.

As you may know, when a starfish is in the water, its five legs move about every which way, seemingly completely independent from one another. But no sooner had I flipped the animal over than its five legs combined forces in perfect coordination to turn it back right side up. When its mouth (on the underside) is facing upward, the starfish knows itself to be in mortal danger, and its body exerts a concerted effort to save it.

It suddenly came to me that there was once a society that behaved very much like the starfish. This was the Buddhist community known as the *sangha,* a group of people who gathered around the Buddha to learn his Law. The *sangha,* in which people enjoyed personal freedom but lived in perfect harmony, was able to exist because its members cultivated in themselves what Buddhism calls the Five Eyes. These can be described as follows:

1. The eye of the flesh is the normal everyday eye that we all have.

2. The godly eye can view the future with scientific accuracy, including matters pertaining to birth and death.

3. The eye of wisdom sees all philosophic truth and discerns the Law behind it. Specifically, it perceives that all phenomena are produced by the fundamental force called *kū* (*śūnyatā*), or the Void, and that they have no permanent form.

4. The eye of the Law perceives the essence of things intuitively, in the same way artists do.

5. The eye of the Buddha possesses compassion, as well as all the qualities and powers of the other four eyes.

When we acquire the visual powers of the Five Eyes, we shall be able to see that everything taking place in this world does so in complete accordance with the law of cause and effect. We will perceive that all existence is interrelated, and we will be able to discern the complicated network of causes that lead to any given result.

To develop the Five Eyes, it is essential for the individual to examine his own body, his own thinking, his own character, his own view of the world—in sum, all the heaven-bestowed qualities that he and only he possesses—and to determine the best and most useful way for him to live. There is a way for children, a way for adolescents, a way for mothers, a way for old people. If everyone knows his own personality and works to make the most of it, there can be peace and harmony for all.

The first goal is to know yourself. If you do not understand yourself, there is little chance that you can understand other people or the world in general.

Machines, let us observe, are not intrinsically bad. The problem lies with people, who rarely make an effort to understand the machinery they use. If we know machines and give them a chance to do what they can do well, they can be valuable comrades and helpers. In the experiment with the four water tanks, for example, a relatively simple machine could control the water level in the fourth tank with no difficulty whatever, despite the lag between cause and effect that throws people off.

In a sense, human beings are merely imprecise machines. A drafting machine can draw a hundred or a thousand perfect circles all the same size, but a human being can't draw even one. If he makes a hundred attempts, each one will be different from the rest. People cannot use gases or liquids with their hands, but machines can handle them by means of pipes and pumps.

Yet tell a machine to unravel a wad of thread, and the machine is at a loss. Machines can perform lowly tasks incomparably better than people can, but they are no match for people when it comes to analyzing the nature of a complicated problem or grasping the total meaning of some train of thought. It is up to people to perceive the nature of the problems confronting modern civilization and to find solutions for them. I, for one, believe that human beings have the strength and capacity to accomplish this.

4

Higher by the Dozen

People frequently ask whether machines are good for mankind or bad. Apparently, some of the machines we make these days are so massive and complicated that they frighten a sizable portion of the population.

An anti-machine man I know takes an extreme position. "By creating machines," he contends, "mankind chose the path leading toward its own destruction. In the course of using machines, people lose their natural hearts and develop cold, mechanical organs to replace them. It does not distress them any more that the automobiles they drive claim as many victims as out-and-out warfare. If someone comes along who is unable to run a machine, they cast him out like so much rubbish."

These charges against mechanized civilization deserve serious consideration. What this man is saying is that, although modern science promised to make life more convenient for us and in some ways did, the machines it developed eventually showed their true colors and set about robbing man of his humanity. Instead of being controlled by man, machines dominate and destroy man.

Since quite a few people have begun to feel that such criticisms may be right, it seems pertinent to review once again just what machines are and what they signify to the human race. In doing so, I must confess that my viewpoint is rather unusual: instead of talking solely about machines, I prefer to line them up side by side with people and compare the respective merits of the two.

An elementary question would be, for example, how do people and machines stack up against each other in size and shape? In answering this, we will note first that there appear to be no size limits on machines: some cover city blocks and others are tiny enough to rest on the palm of one's hand. There are great cranes that can lift tons of coal or steel at once, and there are tiny pincers that lift objects too small to be seen without a magnifying glass. The size of people, on the other hand, is limited to a fairly small range; almost every adult is from 1.5 to 2 meters tall and weighs between 40 and 100 kilograms. It is man's fate not to be able to push out of these size boundaries.

In shape, too, machines can vary tremendously in accordance with their function. If a robot needs a half dozen eyes and arms, for instance, there is no reason why he should not have them. People, on the other hand, all follow virtually the same pattern. We distinguish between handsome or beautiful people and ugly people, but to a robot we would all look pretty much alike.

What about performance? When working properly, a machine can do the work it has been commanded to do with much greater precision than a man. If told to cut a piece of steel or wood so that it is perfectly flat on the surface, the machine will do the work without complaint and will, if necessary, repeat the operation with a high degree of accuracy as many times as is desired. When you instruct a drafting machine to draw circles 50 centimeters in diameter, it will continue to draw circles until the instructions are rescinded, and the circles will all be exactly 50 centimeters in diameter.

Man could have no more faithful or obedient servant than a machine. But a machine can do only what it is commanded to do. If, by stepping hard on the accelerator, you command your automobile to run at a speed of 100 kilometers (about 60 miles) an hour, it will do so until your foot lets up or moves to the brake. Should you happen to fall asleep while driving, the automobile will continue to move forward in accordance with your orders, even though an obstacle should loom up directly ahead. The automobile simply follows instructions; it cannot adjust its behavior to changing conditions. Herein lies the great difference between men and machines. Human beings have both instinct and will; if we sense danger ahead, we can apply the brakes and stop. A machine, which has neither instinct nor will, does not sense danger and would not be able to disobey orders even if it did.

Again, human beings have self or ego, but machines have none at all. Does this lack cause machines to do crazy, irresponsible things? Not at all. It is people, with their egos, who are constantly being led by selfish desires to commit unspeakable deeds. The root of man's lack of freedom (insofar as he actually lacks it) is his egocentrism. In this sense, the ego-less machine leads a less hampered existence.

Machinery is a reflection of the human will. Man seeks something to carry heavy loads for him and, lo, the truck is born. He decides he would like to fly like a bird, only more comfortably, to the other side of the earth, and presently the jet airplane makes its appearance. He longs for a device that at the turning of a switch will clean his dirty clothes, and someone promptly invents the electric washing machine for him.

All this is fine. Life is more convenient with these machines that human beings have willed into existence. Why, then, have machines come to exert a harmful influence on mankind?

One reason is that machinery, while reflecting our will, has a tendency to change people's attitudes toward life. Thanks to efficient new automatic washers, housewives find that their daily chores take much less time than before. What do they do with the leisure time gained? For the most part, they fritter it away staring blankly at television. The television set itself is a convenient machine; it picks up information from all over the world and sets it down before our very eyes. The trouble with this is that if people are able with no effort to acquire a vast quantity of miscellaneous information (and misinformation), they soon stop going to the trouble of thinking for themselves.

When automated machines are installed in a factory, it becomes possible for a worker to turn out an endless stream of products simply by pressing a button or two and occasionally replenishing the raw materials. Once people become accustomed to this mode of operation, they lose the urge to do creative labor or any kind of labor at all. At the same time, they tend to assume that products, so simply produced, ought to be available for the asking; and this leads them to spend beyond their means. It is when this sort of thing happens that critics begin to lambaste machines for converting people into helpless weaklings.

But something is wrong with this argument against machines, as is proved by the fact that certain machines actually encourage human beings to work and improve themselves. Take the piano, for example. Unquestionably it is a machine, but it is one that often inspires its owner to practice and learn. The baby walker and other similar devices stimulate the development of physical or mental skills. Yet no one credits the piano with teaching him how to play or the baby walker with making it possible for a child to walk. The thought would never occur to most people.

So when people tell me that all we need to do to recover our humanity is to eliminate machines and get back to nature, my response is a resounding "I wonder." You understand, I am sure, that I am using the word machine very broadly to refer to any man-made object: a suit of clothes, a cigarette lighter, a watch, a telephone, an electric-light bulb, a heating system, a transport facility—in short, any device or manufactured object that is the product of the human will. It would be very difficult to do away with machines in this sense and go off to live in some secluded spot in the mountains, where nature reigns supreme. Not many people would last more than a few days before flying back to the city and its mechanical convenience. Whether we like it or not, we live in an era when it is necessary to coexist with machines. The main problem is that when men and machines live together men develop traits that they did not have in the premechanical age. The combination of human beings and the devices they have invented has developed into what might be described as a man-machine system. Whether a machine is good or not depends largely on how it functions within this new social complex.

As I have remarked before, machines are by nature free from the drive of egoism that bedevils and imprisons human beings. But when the negative qualities of human beings are multiplied by the negative qualities of a machine, the results can be catastrophic. In ordinary mathematics, a minus multiplied by a minus yields a plus, but this is not true when one is multiplying men by machines. A machine, as we noted, is a reflection of the will of man. If the will it reflects is evil, the machine may well enlarge this evil tens or hundreds of times.

There are people around these days who decry the automobile as an instrument of death that murders countless victims each year. The answer to this accusation is apparent to anyone: there exists no such thing as a vehicle that drives itself, which is what an *automobile* is supposed to be. Always there is a human being behind the steering wheel, and the nature of the newborn entity that comes from crossing a man with a car is what determines whether the machine we call an automobile is a boon to civilization or a murderous weapon. When an automobile careers down a city street at the hands of a speed demon, it can be more vicious than a pack of hungry lions; yet if the speeding vehicle is an emergency ambulance, it may well be saving lives that without it would be lost. An automobile, then, can act as an assassin or as an angel of mercy. This is the way machines are.

Everything is relative. How can we say, as some city dwellers say, that switchblades lead to murders? Knives of similar size and sharpness are used by surgeons to save patients' lives on the operating table. To accuse machines of being good or bad is to miss the point. They can be either or neither.

The truth is that the same duality is found in everything that exists. We could not live without fire, but we cannot live *with* it when it gets out of control. The same is true of water: without it everything would die, but too much of it can be nearly as disastrous.

In the past fifteen or twenty years, there has been so much talk about cigarettes causing cancer that many housewives run their husbands half crazy trying to bulldoze them into giving up the useless weed. Yet I have observed that among the scholars I know, the ones who have developed stomach ulcers are invariably non-smokers. It would appear that tobacco taken in reasonable quantities has the merit of reducing psychological stress.

Nothing in the world is all bad. Nor is anything all good. The world is simply not made that way.

Each of us has a mouth. The mouth is invaluable to us: through it we both supply our bodies with food and communicate our thoughts to others in the form of language. But nothing could be more true than the Japanese saying that the mouth is the gateway to disaster. People have been known to lose status and fortune overnight because of sounds coming from this wayward orifice.

The two hands that we all possess are for most people the source of livelihood. They can perform hundreds, thousands, of functions, not the least of which is to clasp themselves together in prayer to the Buddha. The same two hands, however, are in many ways the most frightening weapons that exist on the face of this earth. Without them, men could not kill, let alone wage war. We would be powerless to strike our fellow man, or choke him, or wave a sword at him, or pull a gun on him, or drop an atomic bomb on him. We wouldn't even be able to slip poison into his drink.

But there is more to relativity than this. Consider, for instance, the concepts of justice and righteousness. Most of you, I feel sure, would automatically say that justice and righteousness are good, but it is a fact that nearly all fights, from squabbles among individuals to full-scale wars between nations, are fought in the name of justice and righteousness. What appears completely just to one group or one nation often appears completely unfair to another group or another nation. At the point where either antagonist becomes so convinced of his own side's rectitude that he is willing to defend it at any cost or sacrifice, there is born into this world a demon that will not shrink even from the idea of killing hundreds of thousands or millions of innocent people. If you do not believe this, try counting the wars that both sides have entered upon for the stated purpose of "preserving peace."

Shakyamuni Buddha taught us that all existence is neutral. This means simply that anything has the potentiality of being either good or bad, and that it is a great mistake to see only one side of the picture. Machines, like everything else, have wide potentialities. Whether they work for good or for evil depends entirely on how we use them.

If it is wrong to attack machines only, it must also be wrong to attack people only. Is there a way out of this dilemma?

Instinct tells me that the biggest problem with machines concerns the intentions—the heart, if you prefer—of the person using the machine. Yet supposing that I, for example, had only the best of all possible intentions, does that mean that any machine I operate will do good? Obviously not, because there are any number of machines that I simply do not know how to operate.

In the future, atomic energy may well be essential to mankind's existence, but, as we all know, it involves grave dangers. Specifically, when gathered in the form of atomic bombs, it has the power to obliterate the human race and all it possesses. But there is little or no chance that I as an individual will decide upon the uses of atomic energy. That will be done in accordance with the will of a large group of people—a community, a society, or a nation. The difficulty here is that the will of a large group is nebulous. You sense that it is there, but you cannot put your finger on it. At the same time, if you attempt to ignore it, it is apt to rise up and slap you down. Whenever an organization is created, there comes into being a new character and will that the individual members did not possess on their own. This new nature is greatly influenced by what I spoke of earlier as the man-machine system, which is born of the interaction between men and their mechanical creations.

Obviously, we would be better off today if we had only good men and good machines—if somewhere along the way we had managed to eliminate or curb the potentiality both men and machines have for evil. The question is, is there any way to do that now?

I think I have discovered one, though not an easy one. The first step, I think, is to try to develop machines that will curb the bad in people. Such machines actually exist even now, a simple example being the safety razor, which has the necessary cutting power to shave a person but is built in such a way that the blade is not likely to cut anything other than the hair being shaved. The safety razor, I might add, is safe in another way: a man in a rage would accomplish little by attempting to use it as a weapon. I realize of course that safety in this case is ensured only by a piece of metal that holds the blade in place. The safety razor does nothing to quiet the rage that causes one man to want to attack another. What we need is a type of machine that will calm the spirit of its user.

As I was pondering methods of incorporating this principle into various types of machines, I received a valuable hint from my secretary Miss Koshida, a charming young lady who always has her wits about her. "Professor Mori," she said one day, "is it possible to make machines that are more expensive by the dozen?"

The idea startled me. Yet it is true on the face of it that if it cost more to produce in quantity, we would produce only that which we strictly need.

The machine—indeed our whole mechanized civilization—is based on the principle that things are less expensive if made in large numbers. Cheaper by the dozen, as we often say. Mechanized or automated production exists for the purpose of producing larger quantities at lower cost. The user of a machine is constantly attempting to coax it into turning out a little more for a little less.

But a graph representing the saving that results from increased quantity assumes the same form as the curve representing the explosion of a bomb, or the progressive contractive force of a hangman's noose in action. A bomb explosion begins with an impulse that sets off a detonator, which is usually attached at the head or the tail of the bomb. From the detonator, the fire spreads to the nearest explosive material and thence throughout the rest of the bomb. Though the reaction is so fast that we hear only one great and seemingly instantaneous bang, the size of the explosion at any given instant can be plotted on a graph, as in Figure 1, where the escalating power is shown by the dotted line curving up toward the right.

In a human being, one burning desire ignites other desires around it, and the fire spreads as in the bomb. The more we feed desire, the more it grows, until it becomes an explosive form of insatiability. The graph of this development coincides with that of a bomb explosion.

I can say one thing with confidence: the crisis of contemporary civilization is that everything seems to be trying to follow the rightward-rising graph toward explosion.

What the Buddha taught us is true: "The cause of all suffering is rooted in desire." The reason why nature, which includes ourselves, has until now been able to grow and flourish in a balanced fashion is that it has followed, not the rightward-rising curve, but the rightward-falling solid curve seen in Figure 1. When the basic hunger and sex urges given to plant and animal life to enable them to preserve themselves are not satisfied, desire asserts itself actively, but if the basic needs are supplied, desire tends to de-

Figure 1

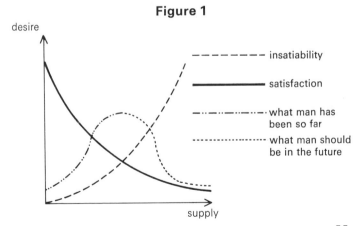

crease. In other words, there exists in nature a desire that knows satisfaction—a desire that does not go beyond certain limits. This moderated desire is the principle that underlies the harmonious workings of nature.

Human beings, sad to say, seem to be trying to change to a form of desire that knows no satisfaction. It is said that when the ancient Romans held great feasts, they would stuff themselves with food and drink, then go to the bath and force themselves to vomit so as to be able to eat and drink still more. I wonder if twentieth-century man does not in his own way go to even more ridiculous extremes to satisfy his desire for material things.

There was once a king who had a retainer who was absolutely and completely loyal. Furthermore, this retainer had the strength of a million men, which he cheerfully employed to acquire for the king anything that the king happened to want. Unfortunately, the king, spoiled by the ministrations of this wonderful servant, formed the notion that the entire world ought to obey his commands. But when he attempted to enforce this principle, the rest of the world attacked and destroyed him, faithful retainer and all.

Our highly mechanized modern world began with tiny, tiny desires. Someone decided that food would be better if there were a fire to heat it with; that the heated food would be easier to eat with chopsticks or a spoon. Thus fire and eating implements came into being. But as our "retainers," the machinery we willed into existence, became more widespread, more powerful, and more loyal, we made the same mistake as the selfish king and allowed our desires to follow the rightward-rising curve. If the earth could provide us with limitless space and raw materials, it might be possible for our material wealth to expand without end. For better or for worse, however, we live within a finite space in which all resources are decreasing in accordance with the rightward-falling curve.

So long as we think of things as being cheaper by the dozen, we will continue to produce in ever-increasing quantities, thus magnifying pollution while at the same time adding to the speed with which our resources are depleted. Eventually there is bound to come a breaking point. If we are to avoid this, we must begin to think in terms of things being more expensive when produced in quantity.

In the long run, what we need most of all today is to reform ourselves. When it comes to the question of how, I think perhaps we could learn a lesson from the butterflies. When insects like the butterfly reach adulthood, they have the strength (economic power, we might call it) to gather enough food to maintain themselves and the capacity (spiritual power) to harmonize with nature. In other words, they are adults not only physically but economically and spiritually as well.

Human beings, on the other hand, usually do not grow in a balanced fashion. As a rule, their bodies mature first, causing them to get married. Only when they are faced with running a household do they realize that they lack the economic strength they need. And it is not until they have established themselves economically that they begin to realize their need for the spiritual ability to harmonize with nature, with machinery, with other people. What we must try to do is change this growth sequence in such a way as to cause young people to reach spiritual maturity first. Physical and economic maturity will follow naturally. Unless we find some way of doing this, I doubt that we can ever create a perfectly harmonious society.

If we are to coexist with machines—and I cannot see how we can avoid coexisting with them—we must develop the spiritual strength needed to control the vast power that a man-machine system possesses. In my opinion, only religion can give us this strength.

My robot's call is loud and clear: "The more mechanized our civilization becomes, the more important the Buddha's teaching will be to us all."

5

Safety Second

The subject of safety is never very long out of the news these days. Any large jet-plane crash or train wreck points up the fact that our twentieth-century system of transportation, which we consider to be quite advanced, is not completely without danger to the traveler. When there is a suggestion that an airplane accident might have been caused by defects in the airplane itself, there is invariably much wringing of hands in the press, accompanied by an outburst of public indignation. Though we insist upon ever greater speed in transport, we are nevertheless outraged when we suspect that manufacturers or public carriers have put speed or economy before safety.

A larger and more chronic problem than mass-transport disasters is the day-in-day-out loss of life in automobile accidents. In Japan alone, approximately 9,000 people died and some 600,000 people were injured in car wrecks in 1978. It is as though we were engaged in a non-ending war. Small wonder that the general public is constantly criticizing the automobile industry for not developing safer cars.

Without doubt one of the great obligations of contemporary

civilization is to make our lives safer. For us to demand this is no more than natural. Yet we must not fool ourselves: the problem of safety involves numerous factors not visible on the surface. Safety first is an appealing slogan, but whether it is a practicable concept or not is questionable.

Automobile manufacturers have spent and are spending untold amounts of money trying to make their products safer, and there has been a good deal of progress along this line. It used to be, for example, that when an automobile traveling at a speed of 100 kilometers per hour (roughly 60 miles per hour) collided with another object, the driver would be thrown forward so violently that he was almost certain to be killed one way or another. Often the steering wheel broke and he was impaled on the steering column. Now, however, collapsible steering columns are in general use, and air bags are available for drivers who feel the need for them.

Some years ago American automobile makers, at the behest of the American government, set out to produce what was called an "experimental safety vehicle" (ESV). The idea was to design a car so safe that if it collided with another object at a speed of 100 kph its driver would suffer only limited injuries. It was thought that the safety devices developed in the course of building the ESV could be incorporated into automobiles all over the world.

This seemed a laudable plan, and it was widely applauded at the time. Critics pointed out, however, that no matter what sophisticated safety devices were invented, there would still be no guarantee of increased safety. Their reasoning went something like this. You can perhaps make a car so safe that the driver escapes with no more than scratches when he runs into a blank wall at a speed of 100 kph. If you make such a car, however, there will invariably be drivers who increase their speed to 120 kph. If somehow you make the car safe at 120 kph, some drivers will push their speed up to 150 kph. It is a vicious circle: so long as cars are driven by people, there is no way to make them absolutely safe.

When asked how he would go about making automobiles safe, one decrier of ordinary safety devices replied, "I would install a pistol in the steering column, rigged in such a way that if the driver exceeded a certain speed limit, the pistol would put a bullet through his brains. This would prevent drivers from speeding and put a stop to the whole safety problem.''

A little extreme? Yes, but there exist cases in which methods based on similar reasoning have succeeded in protecting people from danger. One is to be seen at the famous Lorelei rock, which overlooks the Rhine about halfway down the river's course from Switzerland to the North Sea. Legend has it that boatmen of old were drawn to their destruction by the sweet singing of a siren there. Today many tourists who climb to the top of the rock are astonished to find that there is no fence or guard rail to prevent them from going too close to the edge and plummeting into the river below. But this very lack scares people into maintaining a respectful distance from the danger line, and so far there have been no serious accidents.

As a Japanese, I feel certain that the absence of a protective barrier in a similar location in Japan would cause a public outcry, probably replete with demands for the head of the person responsible. In any case, one will search in vain in Japan for a tourist attraction of this kind that is not amply provided with fences and other safety precautions. But does that prevent accidents? No, indeed. No matter how much money is spent on guard rails, there are always people who climb over them, crawl under them, or find ways around them in order to get to the danger spots. I myself long ago came to the conclusion that it would be much easier to protect people from danger if it were possible to protect people from themselves.

I pointed out earlier that there are two types of desire, that which can be satisfied and that which cannot. The insatiable kind, as illustrated in a simple graph (see page 55) follows an upward curve that terminates in an explosion. The same is true of our demands for safety—and particularly safety in automobiles. The safer cars become, the more we press them for greater speed. It is an escalating process, which is bound to end not in increased safety but in disaster.

But for a moment let us look at safety from another viewpoint. I once asked a fairly large group of people the following question:

"Suppose you were rich enough to do anything you please. What steps would you take to guarantee your safety?" A typical answer read: "Going outside is dangerous. If you board a train, an airplane, or even an automobile, you are liable to be killed or injured in an accident. Even if you're only walking along the street, there's no guarantee that you won't be hit by a runaway truck or struck on the head by something falling from the twentieth floor of a building under construction. What I would do to stay safe is build a big fireproof, earthquakeproof concrete box and provide it with necessary supplies, so that I could live inside it and never have to go outdoors."

In other words, the writer of this response thought he would be safest in an enlarged and glorified version of the concrete pillbox. He is wrong, however, because the human psyche cannot abide such surroundings very long.

Human beings tend to have the illusion that they live through their own strength alone. But, as I pointed out earlier, the truth is that all things animate and inanimate are interrelated and interdependent, and what a human being considers to be his own strength is by no means an independent force. Such is the meaning of the Buddhist teaching that "nothing has an ego."

To live in a pillbox, even a large and luxurious one, would be a violation of this principle. It would also tend to flout the equally important teaching that "all things are impermanent," for to shut oneself up in an isolated box would be to cut oneself off from the normal change and flow of life. From a practical viewpoint, isolation of this kind would most likely cause deterioration of both body and mind. What human being, after all, could thrive in a cage, even a cage of his own making? Confinement within unchanging surroundings and isolation from the movements of the outside would upset any human being's physical and mental balance.

Proof is found in many experiments that psychologists have conducted to determine how long people can stand living in a sealed and isolated space. When scientists conduct such tests, they usually have no trouble finding volunteer guinea pigs. To many people, the idea of receiving pay and three meals a day for doing nothing more than sitting in a closed room sounds like a good deal. So far, however, the longest a person has managed to stand such isolation is eight days. Most volunteers are asking to be let out in much less time—sometimes as little as thirty minutes.

Whether we are conscious of it or not, nothing disturbs us more than to lose connection with the world around us and be cut off from the flow of things.

If neither safety devices nor concrete-clad isolation works, where can we find safety? Having pondered this question for a long, long time, I myself eventually found an answer that satisfied me in chapter 13 of the Lotus Sutra, where the bodhisattvas say:

> We will not love body and life,
> But only care for the supreme Way.

To me this means that when we stop worrying excessively about our physical safety, we find ourselves in the embrace of a more universal safety. We ought therefore to regard our bodies as secondary and concentrate instead on living a full and fruitful life at all times. This does not mean, of course, that we should deliberately expose our lives to peril, let alone the lives of others. The object is to put safety and security in proper perspective. They are important, but not important enough to justify a complete sacrifice of freedom.

The words "We will not love body and life" can also mean "We will willingly forget our body and life." By forgetting oneself and thinking of higher goals, one can find the safety of the Buddha's embrace.

It goes without saying that the teachings of the Buddha are born of a wisdom far surpassing our own. We may think of this wisdom as the "far-reaching wise regard" attributed to the bodhisattva Kannon or as the "skillful wisdom" frequently spoken of by Zen priests. However we describe it, it is a wisdom that encompasses all things and is able to deal with all situations.

When I think of superior wisdom, I am reminded of an embarrassing incident that occurred when I was in high school. As you may have noticed, students rarely exercise their brainpower so assiduously as when they are trying to put some trick over on their instructors. On such occasions, the most dull-witted clod is apt to reveal astonishing ingenuity and powers of concentration.

One day one of our number said, "Men, we are now scholars in an institute of higher learning. We are no longer primary- or junior-high-school students. It is time that we left off childish tricks and devise a caper that has genuine class."

It happened that a Professor Kitazawa was our biology teacher. At each meeting of his class, the good professor did nothing but read to us from a sheaf of aged notes, which we copied down in our notebooks. It was not exactly the same as reproducing by Xerox, but very little more mental activity was involved in the transfer of information from Professor Kitazawa's yellowed cards to our notebooks. To give Professor Kitazawa a jolt, while at the same time lodging a protest against his teaching method, we hit upon the idea of going to the lecture room ahead of time and pulling all the heavy curtains, so as to make the room too dark for him to read his notes.

The bell for class rang. In the classroom everyone was silent as Professor Kitazawa's footsteps approached down the hall. My heart was beating rapidly. How would he react? Everybody held his breath as the door swung open and Professor Kitazawa was silhouetted against the sunlit hallway. He seemed taken aback, if not downright confused, and for a moment I thought lightning might strike.

But nothing happened. Calmly, Professor Kitazawa strolled to the nearest window, pulled back the curtain just enough for himself to see, and began reading his notes as usual. For the Pranksters, it was complete and utter defeat. A great flurry ensued as students rushed to open curtains and get out their notebooks. Professor Kitazawa had the Zen "skillful wisdom," which included the knowledge that he could always get even if he wanted to by giving a test on the contents of that day's lecture.

For some time a few years ago I appeared as a guest on a radio talk program with Ryūji Katayama, a well-known commentator. One day during the broadcast a telephone call came in from a primary school teacher who had phoned to say that, thanks to Katayama's influence, his pupils were much more attentive than they had been in the past. The reason had to do with what Katayama called his "booboo bank." He had a way of fluffing his lines on the program, and to try to break himself of the habit he kept a little savings bank in front of him, into which he dropped a hundred yen every time he made a misstatement. The primary school teacher's students had seen this and challenged him to fork up a hundred yen every time he said something wrong. After a little bargaining, the students agreed to reduce the fine to ten yen, but ever since there had been no more need for don't-talk-to-your-neighbor-while-I'm-speaking or stop-looking-out-the-window-and-listen-to-me. The children were now so eager to catch the teacher in a mistake that they hung on every word he uttered. This teacher, too, had acquired the "skillful wisdom" of Zen.

Upon hearing this story, I resolved to try to achieve the same kind of wisdom, so that I might acquire the ability to see the ultimate reality of the goings-on around me. Not long afterward, I received a lesson on the nature of safety from the robots with which I work.

You've probably noticed that the robots you've seen in futuristic movies all have much heavier underpinnings than the human body. Even if they are designed in such a way as to appear to have legs, the legs are a great deal larger than human legs in proportion to the torso. The reason is quite simple; robots are normally designed to have a low center of gravity, so that they are not easily overturned. Human beings, whose center of gravity is in the general vicinity of the navel, are far more likely to be knocked down by a blow to the body or by the force of a strong wind.

Why is it that our creator gave us less stability than a robot has? Again the reason is simple: the robot is not as a rule required to walk, whereas human beings are. You may have seen robots whose legs moved as though they were walking, but close inspection would reveal wheels or rollers somewhere.

Robots cannot go uphill or downhill. Even on slight inclines they are likely to fall over, and when they do they are unable to right themselves. People, on the other hand, go up and down hills and stairways with ease, and if they feel themselves on the verge of falling they can usually avoid doing so by shifting one leg to a different position. One might say that in human beings a degree of stability has been sacrificed in order to increase mobility. In other words, safety in a standstill position has been reduced to provide safety in a wider range of circumstances. A man is more likely than a robot to be knocked over by a straight right to the jaw, but he is also much better equipped than the robot to jump out of the way of the blow. The kind of safety the robot enjoys because of his low center of gravity is the kind that comes from living in the concrete pillbox we spoke of earlier. For centuries, kings and potentates have been building castles and shutting themselves up inside them for safety. So far, however, there has been no record of a castle that did not eventually fall to attackers. The fact is that mobility is usually safer than stability.

Here in Japan we have, at least for the time being, a unique system of employment in which people who go to work for a given company normally work for that company until they retire. This lifetime-employment system obviously makes for a degree of security unknown in most other countries, but it also carries with it a number of inherent risks for both employers and employees.

Young people about to leave school and go out into the world must decide (if indeed it is not decided for them) right then what sort of company they wish to entrust the rest of their lives to. If they choose wrong at this point, there is little they can do later without incurring severe losses.

When asked where they would like to work, most students reply that they would prefer a large, well-known firm. Why? Because such a company is safe, in the sense that it is not likely to fold even in hard times. Often the student adds that his parents would be happier if he finds a position in a company that everybody knows.

Doubtless a number of young people genuinely feel that a

position with a first-class corporation will give them more opportunity to use the knowledge and skills they have acquired in
school than a job with a small company would. It stands to reason, after all, that large enterprises might offer a chance to do
bigger things than small businesses. In the final analysis, though,
the basic reason why students prefer big companies is the desire
for absolute security.

If I were the president of a large company, I don't think I
would hire young people who seem to be seeking security above
all else. Every company must in the course of its history face a
number of crises, and the people who see it through these are
not the security-oriented drones, but the venturesome souls who
see it as their destiny to remold and improve the company. The
big corporations of our time have arrived where they are today
precisely because they have a high percentage of employees who
are willing to take chances. When a company becomes weighted
down with security-minded hangers-on, its center of gravity falls
—sometimes to the extent that it loses the power to move and
can only stand still waiting for the competition to overtake it. If
a large company that attracts security-seekers is not careful, it can
suffer the fate of the dinosaurs, who lost out in the evolutionary
struggle because they grew so large that their nervous systems
could not carry signals all the way from their brains to the ex-
tremities of their bodies.

In the *sangha* community organized around the Buddha, it
was possible for each member to live the way he wanted to while
remaining in perfect harmony with the group. This is not often
true in modern business corporations. The typical company has
particular goals, and in order to achieve them its officers issue a
stream of directives that flow down from the top to the lowest
levels. When the company's center of gravity is too low, it is
not easy to make sure that these orders are being carried out on
the outer fringes of the organization.

As a rule, people who enter large companies in search of security are far more concerned with protecting their own position
than they are in advancing the company's purposes. They make a

practice of doing what their immediate superiors order them to do and nothing else. Figuratively speaking, such employees have found security by retreating into mental pillboxes. When a company has a preponderance of employees of this kind, it is very easy for a few braver employees to run things to suit themselves, regardless of the company's welfare. This is one of the more severe types of modern corporate illness.

In a small company, if a person works hard, his efforts are soon reflected in increased sales and profits. Conversely, if he loafs, the results show up unfavorably on the company's ledgers. Large companies do not go bankrupt when two or three people fail to work hard. In fact, it is usually difficult to establish a connection between the fortunes of the company and the individual efforts of its employees. This, however, is fundamentally a dangerous situation, because it signifies lack of sufficient communication within the company. If allowed to continue long, it can lead to the corporate equivalent of hardening of the arteries.

If you examine the history of companies that have gone broke, you will find that quite a few of them had built fine new offices and seemed to be in tiptop shape even as the omens of bankruptcy were beginning to become evident. When a company adopts policies that seem designed to demonstrate its own safety and security, the time has come to worry about its future.

In a world where everything is constantly changing and nothing exists except in relationship to everything else, it is a waste of time even to think of trying to find perfect safety. Human beings were not made to travel indefinitely along a smooth, unending expressway. There are no rails along which we can glide effortlessly to infinity. Nor can anyone predict when some obstacle or peril might pop up directly in front of us. We must tread cautiously, step by judicious step. But we must continue to advance, or else we shall stagnate.

Where would the world be if Christopher Columbus had followed the rule of safety first and refrained from challenging the unknown seas to the west? Certainly safety was not foremost in the minds of the astronauts who opened up the way to the moon. The only way in which we can be genuinely safe is to develop behavior techniques that enable us to respond adequately to any change that might confront us. We are safe only insofar as we refrain from loving the body and life and instead devote ourselves to finding the Way of the Buddha.

6

If Pushing Ahead Won't Work, Try Pulling Back

Many years ago, I accepted an invitation to give a lecture in the city of Mihara, in Hiroshima Prefecture. On the day I arrived, it was pouring rain—had been since early morning. From time to time, it would seem to let up a bit, but then another downpour would follow. It was raining when I went to give my lecture, and it was still raining when I returned to the old-style inn where I was staying. I went to bed fairly early, but could not sleep because of the pounding of the rain on the roof and the noise of rushing water in a swollen creek nearby.

Drowsily, I thought, "The rain gathers in the creek, and the creek flows into a river. Where the river's narrow, the water rushes through, but in wider places the flow is slow and gentle. Where the river is deep, the water comes almost to a standstill, but then there comes another narrow stretch and it is forced to flow rapidly again. . . ."

I muttered to myself, "That's the way to be—as adjustable as the water in a stream. If only people were like that! If only *I* were like that!"

There is a saying that water will fill round vessels as well as square vessels. Actually, of course, water will suit itself to vessels of any shape—long, short, flat, wide, narrow, deep, regular, or irregular. What could be more accommodating? Yet the flexibility of water extends to another dimension: when it freezes in a confined place, it has the strength to break out of confinement, even if this means splitting solid rock. To be completely pliant when pliancy is called for and extremely strong when strength is needed —that is true flexibility.

But water has other interesting properties. Without attempting to oppose the laws of nature, it always flows from high point to low point (or, strictly speaking, from point of high pressure to point of low pressure), eventually ending up in the ocean. Yet the ocean is not really a terminal point, because the sun's heat vaporizes water at the ocean's surface and brings it to life again, as it were. The vapor gathers into clouds in the sky and presently falls to earth once again in the form of raindrops. Water thus undergoes a never-ending process of transmigration.

Water frequently occurs in Buddhist metaphors and parables. Perhaps the best-known example is found in the parable of the herbs in the Lotus Sutra, where the Buddha's compassion is likened to the rain falling equally on all plants great and small and nourishing them in accordance with their capacities.

As I lay half asleep at the inn in Mihara, I thought how smoothly the affairs of this world could be handled if each human being had the flexibility of water, if we could all live as freely as flowing water without constantly locking horns with one another.

Unfortunately, that is not the way things work. I spent a few minutes asking myself why it isn't, and suddenly I thought I knew the answer.

Superficially, at least, grains and granulated substances, such as flour, sugar, or salt, behave like water; they will flow from a high place to a lower one, and they will accommodate themselves to either a square box or a round jar. Yet there is an important difference: if you examine flour or sugar under a microscope, you will see a collection of small separate grains, completely unlike the homogeneous liquid that water proves to be under the same microscope. In Buddhist terminology, we might say that water is liquid in both appearance and essence; flour, on the other hand, may at times be liquid in appearance, but in essence it is solid.

The reason why the world's affairs do not flow along as smoothly as water is that human beings are like flour and sugar, rather than water. A crowd of people may flow easily along a hallway or a sidewalk, but its flow resembles that of a granular substance, not that of water.

All of you remember Dr. Gulliver and his travels to strange lands. When his ship was blown ashore in the country of the Brobdingnagians, he saw wheat growing in the fields to a height of ten meters or more. The palms of the people's hands were more than thirty centimeters thick, and the king thought nothing of plopping a full-grown whale into his mouth as an appetizer. Among the Brobdingnagians, Dr. Gulliver was a bug-sized midget, in danger at one point of being swallowed by a baby and at another of drowning in a container of cream.

Suppose you were suddenly to shrink even more than Gulliver, to about the size of a poppy seed. Suppose then that you were to jump into a tablespoonful of salt. What you would see around you then would appear to be great piles of rocks, separated here and there by gaps you could barely squeeze through. Were you to be in this situation for a moment, you would see that the apparent flow of flour and other granular substances is like an avalanche, not like a flood.

This is why these substances do not always flow smoothly. From time to time the grains block each other and get stuck. Remember the salt shaker that won't give salt no matter how you shake it? The grains pile up around a tiny hole and prevent each other from passing through. If you want to unstick the salt, the only thing to do is contrive to move some of the grains away from the hole.

The brick masons of the past made good use of what we might call the stuck-salt principle. If you examine a window in an old European brick house, you will find that the upper part is arched. In building with bricks, it is impossible to line the bricks up in a straight line over an unsupported interval. If they are arched, however, the pull of gravity on them presses them against their neighbors and solidifies the arch structure. The bricks here are fundamentally no different from grains of flour or sugar.

Suppose that instead of becoming very small I become very large, like Gulliver in Lilliput. It is the morning rush hour and I am looking down on the throngs of commuters passing through Tokyo Station on their way to work. To me, they resemble so many ants or poppy seeds, flowing smoothly down the passageways but clogging at the exits, where they all seem to be pushing against each other. The bottleneck is all the worse because these are not ordinary ants or poppy seeds, but ants and poppy seeds burdened with luggage.

It seems to be a general rule that human beings find it difficult to move about without something in their hands. Almost no one travels from his house to his office empty-handed. Everybody is clutching a brief case, a handbag, a paper sack, or some combination of the three. Young women seem particularly fond of enormous shopping bags, which they drape from each hand.

Migratory birds fly south for whole seasons with no baggage. Equally unencumbered are the lions and leopards that cross the African veldts. But when people go places, they carry things with them. "What is man?" The question is difficult, but one possible answer would certainly be "Man is an animal that never goes on a trip without baggage." Because of impedimenta of various shapes and sizes, people in railway stations and other crowded places are all the more likely to bump into each other and get hung up in narrow places.

Alas, the harried commuter lacks the time to reflect philosophically on his predicament. When he finds someone blocking his way, he pushes. If this does not advance his position, he pushes harder.

Pushing comes naturally to human beings. There are even people who argue that nothing worthwhile can be accomplished without repeated pushing. Thus in Japan we find the labor unions and business leaders pushing adamantly against each other each year at the time of the "spring struggle" for higher wages. On almost any day, the government and the opposition are pushing each other in the national Diet. Victims of pollution push against the responsible companies, and the companies push back.

Aside from flowing like water in many situations, granulated or powdered substances resemble water in that in large accumulations they exert a tremendous pressure. Flour pressing against a dam would not be much different from water pressing against a dam so far as the force of the pressure is concerned. When a society that has come up against an impasse presses forward willynilly to a breakthrough, it is as though a dam had broken. Many people can be crushed in the outpouring that ensues.

We usually think of silos as cylindrical towers in which dairy farmers store their hay, piling the newly mown grass on the top as it is cut and removing the daily supply for the cattle from the bottom. Silos are also used, however, for a number of granular or granulated substances, including grain itself, sand, and cement. Sometimes the mouth of the silo gets stopped up and the flow from inside is cut off. This happens because the grains inside become jammed tightly together at the exit. The way to correct this is to insert a stick or pole into the mouth and push some of the grains away. This relieves the congestion inside and makes it possible for the grains to flow freely again. Care must be taken in doing this, however, because the rush of grain from the mouth can be dangerous.

It is a pity, I suppose, that people act more like granular substances than like liquid, but this is a fact that must be faced. The question is, what are we to do when our sandlike flow becomes sluggish and stops?

I can offer only one answer: If pushing forward does no good, try pulling back. At the crowded station exit, if instead of pressing ahead everyone took a step backward, the jam would cease to exist and normal flow would be restored. In the long run, everyone would arrive at his destination a little faster.

When opinions clash head-on, the best solution is for both parties to retreat a step or two. The added distance makes it easier for each side to see and understand the other's position. It should be kept in mind that a demand (push) is likely to be met by a counterdemand, whereas a concession (pull) may well elicit a concession from the other side.

Most of us feel that we know ourselves through and through, but in fact we do not. Because we do not, we have difficulty deciding how to make human relations go smoothly. As often as not, what we actually do has the opposite effect from what we intended.

One afternoon a fly strayed into my laboratory at the university. After a trip or two around the room, he alighted on the window glass and began to beat his wings frantically. Outside it was a warm day in May. The fly could see the clear blue sky through the window and obviously could not comprehend what was preventing him from flying outdoors. The transparent glass was not perceptible to him even though he was pressing himself against it with all his might.

The window was partly open—the fly had flown in through it in the first place. But now the poor creature was so determined to exit through the glass that he did not even think of backing off and taking another look. Taking pity on him, I brushed him toward the open part, but a little later, after I had read another page or two in my book, I glanced up and saw that he was back where he had been before, pushing frantically against the glass. Eventually he exhausted himself and fell dead to the window sill.

People make the same sort of error all the time. We have sufficient visual capacity not to be fooled by transparent glass or plastic walls, but we are extremely prone to the belief that nothing exists in this world save that which we ourselves see. How obtuse! The natural environment in which we live contains an infinitude of objects that our eyes cannot see.

Buddhism warns us not to be misled by what we see with our eyes, hear with our ears, or taste with our tongues. The impressions we receive from our five senses tend to make us ignore the truth that underlies the appearance.

A friend of mine recently shook his head sadly and said to me, "My son has finally broken off from me entirely." The story behind this involved a familiar theme. The father, having seen his son into college, wanted him to go on and graduate, but the boy wanted to quit school and start a small restaurant. The two argued for months, but neither was able to convince the other. Finally, the son left home and set up a night stall on a busy street corner.

I uttered the proper words of sympathy to my friend, but after I returned home I began thinking about what he had said: his son had "broken off" from him. There is something wrong with this, even if it is no more than a figure of speech. The fact is that the process of giving birth to a child consists of separating it from its mother. Once a child is born, his existence is distinct from that of his parents. If the parent wants to talk about the child's "breaking off," he must go back to the moment of birth; it is not something that happens after the child is grown.

Some years ago, at the Japan World Exposition in Osaka, visitors to the zoo were startled by a loud bang. Investigation proved that it had come from the cage of an elephant from Thailand that had just given birth. The noise was that of the baby elephant falling from its mother's body. Despite the alarming crash, the newborn infant was already walking around the cage.

As I shall note again later in another context, if the offspring of wild animals are not able to run with their mothers very shortly after they are born, they are likely to become food for some other animal. Human children are born a little too soon; they must be about a year old before they can walk. Yet from the moment they are separated from their mothers' bodies, they have the ability to stay alive—their hearts, lungs, blood vessels, and other mechanisms necessary to life are functioning independently of their mothers.

To put it in present-day terminology, after birth there is no *hardware* linking parent and child. The single hardware connection, which is the umbilical cord, is cut when the child is born. Were it not, mothers and children would have to live and move about together, like Siamese twins. Life as we live it would be impossible for either.

Yet there is something that links the hearts of parents and

children. What is it? In the language of computers, we would have to describe it as *softwear*—a series of "wireless" links between eye and eye, between ear and mouth, between mouth and ear, that enable parents and children to communicate on a spiritual level even though they are physically independent of each other.

When people speak of a gap between parents and children today, what is meant is that the wireless connections are not working properly. Often, it seems to me, this break in communications results from the inability of the parent or the child or both to recognize clearly that they are indeed separate physical beings. Not perceiving this, they take the connections for granted, whereas these connections are actually so delicate and tenuous that they require constant watching. If both parent and child are conscious of being separate individuals, they are more likely to take care of the spiritual ties that hold them together than if they identify too closely with each other.

The Buddha said, "A foolish man thinks of his children and his wealth as being his own. But even he is not really himself. How can children or wealth be his?"

Shakyamuni Buddha was, in my opinion, a master of paradox, the art of saying something in a way that seems to defy common sense but in fact strikes directly at the truth. We are given to considering our own existence as unshakably real, but Shakyamuni reminds us that even we are not ourselves—that our existence, like that of all other things on this earth, is only provisional, and that the only real existence is *kū*, or *śūnyatā*, the Void, which we cannot see.

That which we can see does not exist; that which exists we cannot see. It sounds paradoxical, but until we have learned the truth of this statement, we cannot perceive ourselves or the world as they actually are.

On the opposite side of every front there is a back; on the opposite side of every back there is a front. One cannot exist without the other. Yet human beings invariably tend to see only the front and to assume that this is all that exists. What is worse, we base our actions on this partial view.

When we push, we must not forget that pulling might be an alternative method. Unfortunately, we do in fact forget. When we have a viewpoint, we must not forget that other people have viewpoints too. Unfortunately, we do in fact forget. Every human being is subject to the illusion that his is the only existence in the world.

Neither we ourselves nor the world around us can be saved unless we learn to see both sides of things, learn to pull as well as push, and learn to maintain a broad and lofty view of the truth. Such, I believe, is the teaching of the Buddha.

7

Seek Happiness in Quality,
Not Quantity

In the world of science, we make great use of something called differential equations. Some of you who have been force-fed calculus in high school or college may be tempted to stop reading at the very mention of this term, but I ask you to bear with me a little longer, because there is a definite connection between differential equations and the teachings of the Buddha.

As you know, there are various kinds of equations in the field of mathematics—algebraic equations, such as $6x = 2x + 8$, differential equations, integral equations, and so on. Differential equations are distinguished from others by the fact that they contain a lot of symbols that look like fractions and contain the letter "d," such as:

$$\frac{dy}{dt}, \ \frac{dx}{dt}, \ \frac{d^2x}{dt^2}.$$

The x or y here may represent population, or temperature, or volume of water, or practically any other variable quantity. The t most often stands for time. For example, if x is the population of Tokyo and t a unit of time, such as a week or a month, the symbol dx/dt will represent the amount the population changes in a given period of time. In other words, dx/dt is the speed of change.

Why do we need troublesome equations involving differentials? Because we cannot accurately describe the natural phenomena that surround us without them. There is practically nothing that can be explained without reference to time.

For a long time I myself wondered why this was so. In the sciences I study, we are usually concerned with what comes after the equations are set up, and I could not see why so many time-oriented equations ought to be necessary. Furthermore, it seemed to me that my teachers were vague in explaining this point.

The day I finally saw the reason for differential equations was the day I first fully understood the meaning of the Buddha's teaching that "all things are impermanent." As you may know, this is one law of the Seal of the Three Laws, which is to say one of the three fundamental principles of the universe. The other two are "nothing has an ego" and "nirvana is quiescence."

Quite a few people take "all things are impermanent" to mean that all existence must eventually die and fade away. This negative aspect figures prominently in Japanese literature of the past, for example. But "all things are impermanent" has a positive sense as well as a negative one. Though the decline and death of human beings is certainly an example of impermanence, so is the birth and growth of human beings. Impermanent is neutral: it simply means "ever-changing," and "all things are impermanent" means that all things are constantly undergoing transformation of one kind or another. Change is a fundamental characteristic of the universe. Shakyamuni discovered this principle twenty-five hundred years ago. Today, we are able, by means of differential equations, to express it in scientific language.

Since constant change is a basic characteristic of the universe, we cannot grasp the real truth of things unless we take the passage of time into consideration. Often when we begin to consider time, we find that ideas we had accepted as true are only provisionally true.

It is often said, for example, that the population of New York

City is 8,000,000. If we are not careful, we tend to forget that the same 8,000,000 people are not just sitting there indefinitely. One of the important facts about New York City, or any other great metropolis, is that the population is always changing—some people dying, others being born; some leaving the city, others moving to it.

Again, when we are told that the Ogōchi Dam, west of Tokyo, has created a reservoir of more than a hundred million tons of water, we are apt to think that the water stays there on a permanent basis. But the truth is that several hundred tons of water flow into the reservoir every day, and a corresponding amount must be allowed to flow through the dam to keep the level of the reservoir constant.

Mr. Kiyoshi Ikebe, an architect whom I greatly admire, once said to me, "Mori, how much thought have you given to the fact that some things in this world change but others do not? Take the Apollo spacecraft, for example. There are things in it that change and others that don't, aren't there?"

I replied, honestly enough, "I'm not sure I see what you mean."

"Well," continued Ikebe, "the computer, the space suits, the shoes for walking on the moon, the food—all those things are new. They result from various changes that have taken place recently. But the fact that the astronauts are seated in chairs is old: people have been sitting in chairs ever since they learned to stand on two feet. No change has taken place."

By "things that change," Ikebe obviously meant things that change in a day or a year or some other span of time measurable on a human scale. By "things that do not change," he meant things that change too gradually for the difference to become evident during a human being's lifetime. Although he did not use the language of Buddhism, his observation points up an important fact about the impermanence of things, which is that the rate of change differs from one phenomenon to the next and may be either very fast or very slow—too fast or too slow for human beings to perceive.

"All things are impermanent" has an important connection with the modern science of ecology, which may be described as the study of all living things.

When I was junior-high-school student, we thought of biology as the study of living things, though the practice in those days was for the teacher to bring stuffed birds or rabbits to class for us to examine and compare with the descriptions in our textbooks. Critics objected that what we were studying was not life but death, and gradually it became the custom for schools to keep live animals or arrange for students to see them at zoos. For purists, however, even this was not enough, because animals in captivity are different from animals in their native habitat. Wild monkeys, for example, do not have cavities in their teeth, but in zoos they sometimes develop them. Gorillas, which normally have no hair in their nostrils, sometimes sprout nose hair in captivity. If we want to know what animals are really like and how they are related to other species, then we must go to the jungle and study them *in situ*.

Ecology is to a large extent an outgrowth of this insistence upon the need for examining the natural state of things. The ecologist is concerned with the relationship between man and all other forms of life that exist on this planet. He attempts to study questions of human population growth and food requirements in terms of the total natural environment.

In line perhaps with the dictum that "nothing has an ego," scientists specializing in control engineering and scientists specializing in ecology have in the past few years grown very close to each other. This is particularly true in the United States of America, where a majority of control specialists seem also to be ecologists.

The point that interests me about this is that almost every time a control specialist or an ecologist opens his mouth, the word "flow" comes out. If you examine scholarly works on ecology, you will encounter "flow" on every page, usually more than once. The essence of flow being change, it seems to me that ecology, one of the most advanced sciences, is trying to tell us exactly what the Buddha told us, which is that "all things are impermanent." This teaching, let me add, was not given us merely as a means of seeing the world more accurately. The Buddha's ultimate purpose in expounding the impermanence of things was fundamentally the message that ecologists emphasize today: if we forget that we are living in a world of change, we are bound to suffer in the long run. The Buddha was telling us, with his infinite compassion, that we must not only recognize the impermanence of all things but also adjust our own lives to it.

If everything in the universe is always changing, it follows that we, as part of the universe, are always changing. Let us make a few observations on how human beings change in reaction to other changes.

Everyone who has ever gone swimming knows that when you first plunge into the water it is much colder than it is after you have been in for a few minutes. The opposite is likely to occur if you take a Japanese bath, which is normally heated to a temperature of about 42° Centigrade (108° Fahrenheit) or more. At first it is painfully hot, but a minute or so after you have immersed yourself in it, you cease to notice the heat.

If you wear glasses, you probably remember that the first few times you put them on they were very distracting. The bridge weighed on your nose, and you were conscious of having something in between you and what you were looking at. After a time, however, you ceased to be able to tell whether you had your glasses on or not. In ordinary parlance, we speak of "getting used to" the glasses or the hot or cold water.

What does "get used to" mean? Why do we "get used to" sensations that are at first unpleasant?

We know from biology that impressions from outside the body are relayed to the brain by means of countless nerves, whose sensitive ends are near the surface of the body. It happens that 80 percent of the nerve ends are stimulated only when some change takes place. Only 20 percent are affected by continued heat, cold, or pain. It follows, then, that the initial shock brought about by a sudden change is much greater than the effect of a steady, constant stimulus. The same principle applies to the eyes, which are more sensitive to moving objects than to still ones. It is for this reason that soldiers nearing enemy lines avoid moving when there is any chance that the enemy is looking, and children playing hide-and-seek remain still when the child who is "it" is near.

How does the eye discern things that are not moving? By keeping on the move itself. Although we are not conscious of it, our eyes oscillate from 50 to 100 times per second. The effect is the same as though the eye were perfectly still and the object being viewed were shaking at the same frequency, thus making itself more noticeable.

Our bodies are made to order for a world in which everything is constantly changing. If we forget this, we are likely to find ourselves in serious trouble.

A certain company president, who was worth several hundred million yen, took a bad spill on the commodities exchange and found that all he had left to his name was five million yen. Convinced that he was ruined beyond repair, he put a pistol to his head and committed suicide.

Not far away from the company president's house lived an ordinary office worker who was constantly short of funds. One night after drinking away his troubles in a neighborhood bar, he bought a lottery ticket, and, the next thing he knew, he had won five million yen—enough to pay all his debts and make a down payment on a new house. He was in seventh heaven.

From these two stories it is clear that the amount of money in hand has nothing to do with whether the possessor is happy or not. To one man, five million yen was a cause for suicide; to the other, it was hope for the future. Happiness always depends on the degree and direction of the change that has taken place, for human beings are far more sensitive to change than to the normal routine of life.

I have a young friend named K, who graduated from college, married, and had two children while still living in a one-room apartment. When K managed to move into a small house of his own, with three rooms and a dining-kitchen, he was the happiest man in Japan. But our sensitivity to change does not allow us to rest long. After five or six years, K was complaining bitterly about having to live in such cramped quarters. And at this stage nothing short of a house twice as large would have satisfied him. K was doing what most people do: he was seeking happiness through quantitative change. No doubt he had come to believe, as most people believe, that increased quantities of material possessions mean happiness.

During the last three decades, Japanese society as a whole has come to believe that happiness means more of everything. After fighting a war in which they lost practically everything, the people of Japan were forced to try to produce as much food, as much clothing, as much of anything as they possibly could. As time went on, they learned that by producing more and more washing machines, television sets, automobiles, and so on, they could become richer and richer. There developed a subconscious belief that quantitative improvement meant increased happiness.

For business enterprises, increased production as a rule brought increased profits. If a company's sales increased 18 percent in a given year, the management usually resolved to equal or better that growth in the following year. For a long time, the quantitative growth that resulted satisfied everyone, but eventually people began to suspect that there was more to happiness than a higher material standard of living. Recently, many Japanese have become aware that it is possible, even in the midst of plenty, to be unhappy. Others have begun to see an even more basic fact, which is that quantitative improvement simply cannot go on at the same pace forever.

Look what happens when a company increases production by 18 percent each year for a number of years. Assuming production at the starting point to be unity (1), the increase is as follows:

1st year	1×1.18	$= 1.18$
2nd year	1.18×1.18	$= 1.39$
3rd year	1.39×1.18	$= 1.64$
4th year	1.64×1.18	$= 1.94$

5th	year	$1.94 \times 1.18 = 2.28$
6th	year	$2.28 \times 1.18 = 2.70$
7th	year	$2.70 \times 1.18 = 3.18$

In fourteen years, the total would be more than ten times the original output. Since the world's resources, not to speak of its markets, are limited, it is obvious that an annual production growth of 18 percent cannot be maintained indefinitely.

People do not find life worth living unless they experience change, but change in the form of quantitative growth is limited by the fact that resources are finite. Excessive quantitative growth is self-defeating and self-destructive. What, then, are we to do?

This is one of the biggest problems confronting the world today. As I was considering it, it occurred to me that what we call happiness and sorrow are connected with the purpose of our being. The Buddha created us in such a way that if we are in tune with the purpose he had in mind for human beings, we are happy, but if we are not in tune with this purpose, we are sad. This is the way butterflies and dragonflies are made—why should it not be the same with people?

I asked myself at this point just what happiness and sadness are for me. If someone gives me a good meal and I eat enough of it to satisfy my bodily needs, I am happy. Food and nourishment are necessary to maintain a person's health. Once I have discovered that eating is pleasant, I want to eat again. It is also a pleasure to fulfill the sex urge in the proper way; for this is the means whereby we make better children and grandchildren.

On the other hand, if we collide with something or break an arm or a leg, we experience pain, and once we understand pain, we take whatever precautions we can to avoid it. Truly, human beings are well designed. Just how well can be shown by using a hypothetical robot. A robot can theoretically be wired in such a fashion that it finds pleasure in pain and pain in pleasure. It can be made, for example, so that it objects to being fed (which is to say, being given a new supply of electric power, which is its nourishment). Conversely, it can be designed in such a way that

that it will beat its head against a wall until it destroys itself.

In view of all this, we must realize that if we attempt to satisfy our human desire for change with nothing more than quantitative improvement, we shall be moving in the direction of suffering, because there is a point beyond which quantitative growth is impossible. What we must aim at is qualitative change, which can continue forever.

My point is that it is wrong to think that, since we made 100,000 refrigerators last year, we ought to be able to make 120,000 this year. Instead of making more and more refrigerators, we ought to be manufacturing something completely new that can be made with the same amount of steel as 100,000 refrigerators.

The question, then, is what to make. If it is simply a matter of producing more of the same product—a quantitative change—you can do that without thinking. But if you are seeking a qualitative change, you must use your head. This is what is called creating. Merely repeating the same process leads to unspeakable sorrow, but creating something new leads to indescribable joy.

Creation is the greatest source of joy in the world. Without it, life would be unlivable.

The great Japanese tea master Sen no Rikyū (1522–91) created a whole aesthetic system around the mere drinking of tea. Starting with the mechanical processes involved—putting the powdered tea into a tea bowl, pouring hot water over it, stirring until the powder is dissolved, drinking the tea—he introduced a code of etiquette and an aesthetic ideal that lifted the tea ceremony to a spiritual level approximating that of religion.

Rikyū is particularly famous for developing the concept of *wabi*, which is often translated as "simplicity" or "rusticity," but which I think of as the wisdom required to find riches in poverty, beauty in plainness, much in little. Only if a person has creativity can he follow in the footsteps of Rikyū. When uncreative people practice the tea ceremony, it disintegrates into a formalistic exercise devoid of beauty or spiritual meaning.

That is what has happened to the tea ceremony in modern Japan. Today, practitioners of the cult worry far more about the quality of the tea vessels than they do about the spirit of the ritual. Lip service is paid to *wabi,* but a "simple, rustic" tea bowl is usually not deemed "simple" and "rustic" enough unless it was made by a famous ceramist and purchased at a cost of millions of yen. What was once *wabi* is now a self-centered form of prissiness. Our lives have become so Westernized in the past century that Rikyū's system no longer fits in with them, and for that reason it is dying. To revive it now would require true creativity.

Yet to create something completely new requires a knowledge of that which is old. Often a new creation can be made simply by reversing the old.

You probably think of a truck as a vehicle on which cargo is loaded for purposes of transport. But why couldn't a truck be designed so that the cargo is suspended underneath rather than loaded on top? As a matter of fact, an upside-down truck of this sort *has* been designed, in the form of what is known as a straddle carrier. In the case of a conventional truck, the cargo must be lifted, moved sideways, and set down on the floor of the vehicle, but the straddle carrier literally straddles the cargo and lifts it a short distance off the ground in order to move it.

This is not really a new idea. Centuries ago, when Toyotomi Hideyoshi (1536–98) forced his vassals to supply huge rocks from their provinces to build the colossal castle at Osaka, the vassals had little trouble acquiring the rocks, but a great deal of trouble transporting them by boat to Osaka. Eventually someone saw that their problem was that they were trying to load the rocks on the boats, when what they ought to be doing was load the boats on the rocks. When the rocks were loaded on deck, the center of gravity rose to the extent that the boats were dangerously top-heavy. If the rocks were attached to the bottoms of the boats, however, the center of gravity was stabilized, and the weight of the rocks was reduced by the buoyancy of the water. Reexamining the traditional can often lead to the creation of a completely new device or method.

SEEK QUALITY, NOT QUANTITY 87

The Buddha said, "All things are constantly changing. Be ye diligent." To me, this means that since we live in a world that is being transformed from moment to moment, we must work at being creative, so that we can improve our lives in a qualitative sense. This is the way to find happiness.

8

From Paradox Comes Wisdom

"There's nothing like a dull knife for cutting your finger."
"If you want to remember, make sure you know how to forget."
Statements like these are called paradoxes. Though they seem to defy common sense, they emphasize one aspect of the truth. The world does not lack people who find paradoxical expressions indirect and annoying, but I personally happen to be particularly fond of them. They seem to me to have more eloquence than more direct ways of expressing the same idea.

Common sense tells us that when a knife or a razor blade is very sharp, we can cut ourselves to the bone merely by rubbing a finger against it by accident. A dull knife is not likely to cut so easily. Mother is not wrong, therefore, when she says, "This butcher knife is much too sharp for children to play with." On the other hand, there is another problem that this warning does not cover.

When we say we have peeled an apple or carved a woodblock plate with a knife, we rarely stop to think that the knife was able to perform the task in question only because we exercised complete control over it with our fingers, hands, and wrists. When we do work of this kind, a very sharp knife moves smoothly in the direction we desire, but a dull knife is likely to catch here and there or to go off on some unforeseen tangent. It is when the knife is difficult to control that we are most likely to slip and cut the hand that is holding the apple or the wood block. This is the situation where the paradox stated at the beginning applies; and the paradox gains depth of meaning because it takes into consideration not only the knife itself but also the manner in which we control it.

Common sense is necessary if only because it makes communication between people possible. If there did not exist certain premises tacitly accepted by us all, we would not be able to talk to each other. On the other hand, it sometimes happens that by relying on common sense alone we miss an important point. That is where the paradox comes in—it calls our attention to the exceptions that prove the rule and thereby sets us to thinking. It thus gives us extra insight, over and above common sense. It seems to me that this added insight—this mental reserve force, so to speak—is what Buddhists call "virtue" or "merit." It is no coincidence, I am sure, that the Buddha made ample use of paradoxes in his sermons.

Shakyamuni said, "When you have severed all attachments, everything in the world becomes yours." Another way of saying the same thing is, "If you would make everything your own, you must want nothing."

A lot of "practical" people would dismiss this as nonsense, but I can see the truth of it merely from observing the students in my class. I have often said to students, "If after you've graduated from college you keep trying to remember everything you've learned, you won't accomplish much in life."

I don't say this to freshmen, of course, because if I did they would not study. But after a serious student has made his way through four years of college, he is ready to learn that in order to remember he must forget.

I can explain what I mean by comparing the brain of a robot with that of a man. In making a robot's brain, you start with a computer and teach its memory system each fact it must know, fact by fact, one thing at a time. How different the learning process is with human beings, who already have brains! Instead of one fact at a time, people are constantly observing, or learning, a large assortment of facts. If I see a dog, for example, I remember that it walks on four legs and has a pointed face with which it makes a noise that sounds like "Arf, arf!" Just after seeing the dog, I will possibly also remember that it was a white and black spaniel that wagged its tail and pranced about playfully, occasionally sniffing impatiently or rubbing itself affectionately against my leg. After a few months or a year, however, I will have forgotten the details and remember only the main features. When I have seen several dogs, my mind will have abstracted the features that it associates with the word "dog."

Suppose that I then see a horse. I say to myself, "The horse runs on four legs like a dog, but is several times as big as a dog and has an even longer face." I file the horse away beside the dog in a mental drawer labeled quadrupeds.

Over a period of time, apples, oranges, and ripe persimmons come to share a drawer in my mind that contains round fruits with a sweet flavor. Sea bream, carp, and sardines are in a drawer for creatures that swim with a graceful swaying motion through the water.

In the study of engineering, which is my profession, I must learn a number of theories and fixed values. I need to know, for example, that the distance around a circle is 3.1416 times the diameter of the circle, and that when a body falls from a height it has an acceleration of 9.8 meters per second per second. As time goes on, the figures that I need to remember become more numerous and often more complicated. Must I continue to try to memorize them all? Heavens, no! The most common ones, such as pi or the rate of acceleration due to gravity, can be memorized in grade school, never to be forgotten, but there is a limit to what can be remembered accurately. To attempt to build a bridge or a ship or a jet plane on the basis of remembered figures for the relative strength of various building materials would be sheer insanity. Such figures are available in any number of manuals, and all the expert need keep in mind is the *order* of the figures (that is, whether they are on the order of ten or a hundred or a thousand). The fact of the matter is that by forgetting the exact values of various quantities, you make room in your head for a number of more important facts. The person who is good at forgetting non-essentials is likely to be good at remembering essentials (provided he is good at remembering *anything*, that is). Conversely, the man who tries to remember everything is apt to end up remembering nothing.

Unlike the robot, whose brain is built up piece by piece from bits of information that must be remembered, the human brain is faced with the problem of deciding which among a vast variety of incoming signals need to be remembered and which can be forgotten.

In my opinion, Shakyamuni Buddha used paradoxical expressions because of their ability to startle us into thinking. He used them specifically when he was trying to teach us that which he most wanted us to learn, which is to say the ability to see ourselves as we really are.

We are inclined to say, without thinking very much about it, that man is the "lord of creation." As I was washing my face the other morning, however, I began wondering about this.

Late the night before, I had returned from a visit to Kyoto University's Primates Research Institute, which is in Inuyama, north of Nagoya. This establishment, which sometimes collaborates with my team of researchers working on robots, has a lot of monkeys, and as I was brushing my teeth I remembered how some of the monkeys had bared their white teeth at me the previous evening when I had walked up to their cage.

I stopped brushing and thought, "We go through these motions with the toothbrush every morning with the idea that we're making our teeth stronger. But I never heard of a monkey, or a dog or cat for that matter, brushing his teeth. Nor did I ever hear of one of them having a cavity in a tooth. I suppose the only thing that's getting stronger from all this tooth brushing is the arm I use to push the brush. The reason I have to keep doing it is that if I don't my teeth will decay. Am I really the 'lord of creation'?''

When you consider the matter, people are actually inferior to animals in many ways. If we eat too much, we have gastroptosis; if we lift something too heavy, we are likely to sprain our back or develop a hernia. Animals, who walk on all fours, don't have problems like these. Furthermore, most of them can live among trees on the sides of mountains, whereas we have to be on level ground.

It happens that I play the flute, and so I know that in order to play the instrument well one must inhale from the abdomen, as do marathon runners and people who sit for hours in Zen Buddhist meditation. It is not easy to learn to breathe this way— for a long time, no matter how I tried I continued to inhale from the chest. Finally, Masao Yoshida, flutist for the NHK Symphony Orchestra, explained the secret to me. "First," he said, "you get down on your hands and knees. Then open your mouth, stick out your tongue like a dog, and start saying 'h—a—a, h—a—a' slowly. As you do so, gradually stand up, without changing your way of breathing. You will find that you are taking in air from the abdomen, in proper fashion.''

Of course. If you stand on all fours, part of your weight hangs from your shoulders, and their position is fixed, which makes it practically impossible to breathe from the chest. When you think of it for a moment, people were originally intended to walk on all fours. If we actually walked that way, the front of our body would be strong enough to support the stomach, and there would be no great burden on the bones forming the hinge at our hips. Had we been designed to walk erect in the first place, presumably there would have been some sort of suspension for the stomach, and the spinal discs could have been no stronger than would be necessary for that.

What actually happened was that our ancestors gradually contrived to walk erect. This freed their two forelegs, which then became arms. With their arms, men learned how to build fires and cook food, and this is why we have cavities in our teeth today.

Did all our troubles begin when our early forebears took it upon themselves to walk on their hind legs? I would not presume to answer that question. All I can say for certain is that when man began to stand erect he became a very special kind of animal, different from his nearest relatives in several important respects.

I am all in favor of man's taking pride in being the "lord of creation" and accepting the responsibility that goes with the honor, but I cannot refrain from sounding a sobering note. We can get into serious trouble if we delude ourselves into believing that we are "lords of creation" because the lions and tigers and bears and earthworms that make up the rest of the animal kingdom respect us and acknowledge our primacy. We had best make sure we know our own weaknesses—such, for example, as the relative inability of our instincts to carry us through in all circumstances.

It remains true that we have the use of two hands, by virtue of which we not only made ourselves liable to dental cavities but also gained the ability to brush our teeth and thereby enlarged our brain power to some degree. If we use our arms and our brains to the full, there is no reason why our lives need be less well balanced than those of four-legged animals living by instinct.

We have, after all, many advantages over lesser beasts. One of the most important is our ability to see—perceive—things that other animals cannot see. Whether we actually use this ability to the full or not determines to a large degree whether we lead happy lives or not.

This leads me to a paradox found in the Sutra of Meditation on the Bodhisattva Universal Virtue: "Closing my eyes, I see the buddhas, but when I open my eyes I lose sight of them."

This is the key to man's problem with his powers of vision. If he can "see" what there is to be seen when his eyes are closed as well as what is there when they are open, he can find the superior wisdom of the enlightened one.

Figure 2

If you were asked which of the two lines in Figure 2 is the longer, you would probably pick the uppermost line. The two lines are actually of the same length, but the addition of the outward-opening arrows makes the line at the top seem to extend farther than it does. We are fooled by the outer contours of the total object, which make a stronger impression on our optical nerves than the lines themselves. In a sense, vision begins with distinguishing objects from other objects.

The difficulty here is the constant danger that strong contours might obscure from us the true nature of the object we are viewing.

The surface of the human body is formed of skin. Skin therefore can be regarded as the boundary between ourselves and the space around us or between ourselves and other human beings. To partition a person from his surroundings is not the only function of skin, however, as we can see from examining the nature of skin a little more closely.

Under a microscope, skin proves to be formed of countless cells, on the outer sides of which are cell walls. Cell walls divide us from other things, just as they divide apples or peaches or onions from the great outdoors. The role of the cell walls is much more involved than this suggests, however, because they also have the function of admitting to the body that which the body needs and keeping out that which it does not need. Their ability to distinguish between the two is remarkable: sodium and potassium look very much alike to the human eye and in fact differ only by the presence or absence of an electron; yet cell walls distinguish between the two.

Within our bodies, our kidneys perform the function of cleaning our blood. When the soiled blood passes through them, they are careful not to strain off red or white corpuscles or health-giving proteins, but waste substances are transmitted to the urine, in which they are ejected from our bodies. The selection of waste to be removed is carried out by cell walls.

One might say that the whole mystery of life is embodied in the cell wall membrane. This membrane, far from merely setting human beings (or apples or peaches or onions) apart from other entities, acts as the vital link between the life that is inside the body and the world that is outside.

In general, what I have elsewhere called "separate types," by which I mean objects that are cut off from and independent of other objects, nevertheless exist by virtue of their connection with these other objects. For this reason, if our bodies were tightly wrapped in vinyl or some other substance that completely insulated our skin, we would soon die.

If we fail to perceive the connective function of skin, we have not understood the true nature of skin. But unless we are on our toes, our eyes' propensity for seeing contours will mislead us.

Living bodies are not the only entities that can be regarded as separate forms. If we examine the fashion in which products are distributed in our modern industrial civilization, we shall find separate companies performing a number of distinct functions: a steel company imports iron ore and turns it into steel plate; an automobile company turns the steel plate into a car; a transport company carries the car to the market; and a trading company sells it. Each of these companies is, from outward appearances, a separate form or entity.

When goods flow from one separate type to another, the points of contact (i.e., the borders) between the various forms become vitally important. It is at these junctures that checks must be made to ensure that quantities are correct and defective products have been removed. Each company involved must realize the need for good working connections with the other companies, not only to protect its own interests but also to make certain that the flow of goods to consumers is smooth. Lack of cooperation or coordination at the points of contact can lead to serious malfunctions and to losses for all concerned.

Since we never have any way of knowing exactly what the future will bring, it behooves all of us who are separate types to have some sort of reserve laid aside in case we have to adapt ourselves to drastic changes. The human body maintains a reserve of flesh and fat just in case it becomes necessary to go without food for a while; rivers have depths where excess water can accumulate for later drainage. We keep reserve ink in our fountain pens, reserve gas in our cars, reserve rice in our larders. Companies have warehouses for reserve supplies or products.

Broadly speaking, there are two kinds of reserves, or savings. One involves laying in a large supply that is later dispensed little by little, like the fuel in a car or the rice in a bin. The other type involves accumulating a quantity bit by bit for subsequent disposition at once; this is what is done with garbage pails or the human bladder.

Look at your savings-account passbook, and you will probably see evidence of both types of reserves. A big amount goes in when you receive your salary, and this is gradually used as you pay various monthly expenses. But you are saving a certain amount each month that will ultimately be disbursed in one lump sum, perhaps as the down payment on a house or car.

The scarcer the world's resources become, the more necessary it is for us to manage our reserves effectively. Yet how often we fail to do this! When there arises a shortage of some product, instead of throwing their inventories on the market, merchants increase their stockpiles in the hope of selling for still higher prices later. In an opposite fashion, when we hear a bit of gossip that is likely to cause an unfortunate stir if it gets about, instead of keeping it to ourselves as we ought to do, we broadcast it as fast as we can.

What we need to do now, I think, is close our eyes and try to see the truth. What we will perceive, I believe, is that unless we consider the other fellow and his viewpoint and make an effort to establish good relations with him, we ourselves will eventually come to grief. The heart that can read this message has that extra wisdom—that mental reserve force—that I spoke of earlier.

One rainy day, I was walking up the stairs of my third-story laboratory with one of my students. "Look," I said to him, "your foot leaves a print where you step. Theoretically, that footprint marks all the space you need. If that remained and the rest of the stairway were taken away, could you climb the stairs?"

"No," he answered. "I'd be so afraid of slipping off and falling that my body would tighten up and I wouldn't be able to walk."

Such is the need for the "reserve" space around the actual area we tread on.

When we reached the laboratory, we saw a row of sparrows perched on a telephone wire outside the window.

"How," I asked, "can they go to sleep on a thin, unstable wire like that when we don't really feel at ease in a swinging hammock?"

The student made a very sensible reply: "They are comfortable because they have strength in reserve. After all, they know that even if the wire dropped out from under them, they could still fly."

It was in order to give us the same kind of reserve strength that the Buddha chose to speak in paradoxes and thereby to show us a world that we cannot see with common sense alone.

We have all heard of the well-prepared student who was so afraid of failing an examination that he clammed up and actually failed it. We've heard, too, of the merchant who was so afraid he himself might lose some money that he backed out of a deal at the last minute and brought disaster on himself and all his partners. In this noisy bustling world of ours, we need all the reserve strength the Buddha can give us, not only so that we can exploit our own talents, but also so that we can help our companies and the society in which we live to realize their full potentialities.

9

Active and Passive

One of my scientific colleagues, Ryūichi Tomiya, is not only an expert engineer but also a first-class artist, whose paintings appear in international exhibitions and are quick to be sold whenever he holds a one-man display in Tokyo. Tomiya is one of those rare persons with both scientific and aesthetic acumen. When he designs a mechanical device, it is invariably something to behold.

Some years ago Tomiya put together a little contraption, a simple vehicle with three wheels and a propeller. What is unusual about it is that, although it has no motor, when the wind blows it moves, not with the wind, but against it. Tomiya called it the Wind-defying Tricycle.

If the little cart had a motor of its own, it would be in no way remarkable, but it hasn't so much as a battery, let alone an engine. Yet Tomiya has geared it in such a way that when the wind starts blowing, the little device moves cheerfully straight into it, to the astonishment of observers.

In the world of engineering, if a machine has a built-in motor we call it "active," and if it has no motor we call it "passive." From the technical viewpoint, Tomiya's Wind-defying Tricycle is unquestionably of the passive type, but since it uses the wind to move against the wind, in operation it has a certain active aspect.

When I first saw this little machine, it set me to thinking. Perhaps we ought to reexamine our concepts of active and passive. It might not be worth the bother if they were only technical terms, but they are, after all, words that are used not only by scientists but in everyday conversation as well.

We sometimes tell a young man, for example, to "be more active," meaning that he should go about his business with more vim and vigor. Someone else we might criticize by saying, "His way of life is too passive." "Active," in cases like this, has connotations of strong will, aggressiveness, virility, and the ability to see a task through. "Passive" implies that a person does not act until he is commanded to, that he is lacking in ambition, imagination, or drive. When you see a mother leading her child by the hand, you consider the mother to be the active partner in the relationship and the child to be the passive partner. Or if a couple is walking arm in arm down a street in Tokyo after dark, you might assume that the man is the active party and the woman the passive party, who is merely complying with his wishes.

But consider a different situation. Suppose that I, while seated at my desk, clasp a pencil between the palms of my two hands and move it from the right to the left side of the desk. A very simple operation, right? Yes, but consider it as a problem of control. Did my right hand carry the pencil across, or did the left hand? Can we consider the right hand to have been active and the left hand passive? Or is it the other way around? Or again are both hands to be thought of as active? If you make a robot perform the same action, you will begin to understand the problem. Assuming that you make both of the robot's hands active, if you do not adjust the push of one to the pull of the other, you will end up with a pencil that has been either crushed flat or torn to splinters.

To keep the left and right hands of a robot balanced when they carry a single object is a very difficult task. Think of it as trying to manage a husband-and-wife team both of whom are of an active temperament. He says, "Let's go this way." She says, "You can do as you please, but I'm going that way." Result: either collision or separation.

Yet human beings have no trouble at all making their two hands work together. Nor does a well-matched couple have difficulty cooperating with each other. The secret lies in finding the right balance between the active and the passive. For a man and a woman to be able to create a more rewarding life together than they can separately, a remarkable mechanism must be brought into play.

When we are not thinking, we are apt to say that an active way of life is good because it is progressive, whereas a passive way of life is bad because it is stagnant or retrogressive. Actually, however, the active brings the passive into existence, and vice versa. The best way of life involves a combination of the two. That everything, but everything, moves smoothly when there is harmony between active and passive principles is evident all around us.

As I was thinking this thought, I picked up my coffee cup and took a leisurely sip. In other words, I grasped the handle of the cup, lifted, and the whole cup rose in response to this action. If the side of the cup opposite the handle had said, "I'm not going—I'm staying right here!" presumably the cup would have broken. An important principle is concealed herein.

What I lifted was only the handle of the cup. In genial response to my action, the handle came along, and the other parts of the cup—not only those immediately next to the handle, but those on the other side as well—followed along with equal amiability. Thanks to their passivity, I was able to sip my coffee. As I thought this over, the coffee cup began to seem like a very accommodating little creature, or group of creatures, always willing to do my bidding. When you consider it, our lives are full of tools whose sole reason for existing is to be of use to us. Your desk, your chair, your lighter, your ashtray, your glasses—all are made for your use. Every dish, every spoon, every fork, every knife is made in a form usable by the human animal, which is to say by a biped standing an average of about 1.60 meters, weighing 60 or so kilograms, and having two arms, two frontward-oriented eyes, ears on either side of the head, one nose, and one mouth.

If all these dishes and utensils had to be made for animals having different proportions, their form would have to be very different. A flat plate may be all right for a human being to eat from, but it is no good for, say, a cocker spaniel trying to keep his beautiful long ears clean.

Every housewife is beholden any number of times each day to the water faucet attached to her kitchen sink. What would she do if the faucet were not designed and placed with her dimensions and needs in mind—if it were, for instance, a meter higher on the wall, or if its handle could not be adjusted without a wrench?

The more you look about you, the more you will be convinced that just about everything is waiting to do your will.

The small teapot we use in Japan for everyday tea (as opposed to ceremonial tea and British-style tea) is interesting in that its handle projects at a right angle to the spout. When a person dressed in a kimono and kneeling on tatami pours tea, large movements of the body are out of place. If it were necessary, for example, for the pourer of the tea to raise his (or more likely, her) elbow, the kimono sleeve would move away from the body, and the unsightly opening under the armpit would be visible. With the traditional teapot, the tea can be poured with a mere twist of the wrist.

By way of contrast, the larger pots used in the West for tea and coffee normally have handles directly opposite the spouts. These vessels are suited to Western-style clothing and to a setting in which everyone sits in chairs around a large table. In these circumstances, if a Japanese teapot were used, the server would have to go around the table and pour for each person, but with the Western utensils the housewife can, without leaving her chair, serve her husband and everyone else.

My view is that tools and machines are all in a sense extensions of or substitutes for our hands and feet and ears and eyes. We can scoop water up with our hands and drink it, but in doing this we usually spill about half the water. How much more efficient to replace the palms of our hands with a cup or bowl, which has the added advantage of being able to handle liquids too hot for the hands to touch! With my naked eye, I cannot tell one person from another at a distance of a hundred meters, but I can easily do so if I use binoculars or a telescope. Tools and machines are means of transferring our bodily functions away from our bodies.

Human beings, or for that matter almost all beings born into this world, are endowed at birth with the functions needed for life. These functions come into play and develop as they are needed. Nearly all living creatures get through life with these functions alone, but human beings have from sometime in the past had what is called civilization, and civilization is a way of life in which certain bodily functions are separated from the body.

In the prehistoric past, human beings who lived in very cold climates were no doubt covered with warm fur, but when they began wearing clothes the fur became superfluous and stopped growing except in particular areas. The function of keeping the body warm was transferred from the fur, which was part of the body, to clothing, which is not. With this transfer, it became possible by merely changing clothes to adjust more effectively to the prevailing degree of warmth or cold.

It is also true that in prehistoric times the soles of men's (or their ancestors') feet were thick and leathery, like those of monkeys, but in time the function of protecting the bottoms of the feet was transferred to footgear. As a result, people are now too tenderfooted to walk shoeless except in very limited situations. This does not mean, however, that the purpose of transferring bodily functions away from the body was to make us weaker. On the contrary, primitive man's persistent effort to make tools take over various functions from his body may be seen as an attempt to broaden his other functions or acquire new ones.

Japan's oldest history is the *Kojiki* (Record of Ancient Matters), completed in 712. Until the stories and myths and poems included in this work were written down in the form we see today, they were preserved by oral tradition. A special class of "storytellers" passed them down from generation to generation. One supposes that these storytellers, living in an age when paper and writing were unknown, had better memories than we have today. By entrusting the function of remembering, or a large part of it, to paper and the written word, we may perhaps have weakened our own ability to recall the past, but the memories stored on paper are thousands, millions of times more detailed and complete than what the ancient storytellers were able to memorize. In the same way, the men of prehistoric times may possibly have had stronger legs than ours, but their ability to get around was far more circumscribed than what we have acquired by ceding the functions of our legs to automobiles.

If we think along these lines, many things that we are accustomed to overlooking leap suddenly into view. We might say now, for example, that tools and machines, while appearing to be separate from us, are in truth only functions that have been cut away from us, but are essentially a part of us. When this connection is established, the idea that machines are enemies who threaten to dominate and destroy man is seen for the absurdity that it is. If tools and machines were really trying to harm society, it would be as though we ourselves were using our arms and legs to damage society.

Which brings me, by a roundabout route, to at least one conclusion. In general, the attempt to decide which hand, left or right, is active and which is passive is based on false premises, as is the question of man versus the machine. If we had not created an artificial distinction where none exists—chosen, that is, to regard as two something that is only one—the problems referred to could not exist. This conclusion seems to me to accord perfectly with the teachings of Shakyamuni Buddha and with the general train of Buddhist thought.

In my opinion, the Buddha's most basic teaching is that we must not consider as separate that which is one. To commit this fallacy is what is called in Buddhism sinful or unclean.

There are invariably those who object that the real world is composed of many people and many things, which can only be regarded as plural. As a student of mine once insisted, ''There are my parents and I, you and I, my friend Andō and I. We all have separate bodies. And our bodies are separate from the tools and machines we use. That is the way things are, and you cannot deny it.'' I contend, in face of this, that the student thinks what he thinks because he lacks the eye to perceive the links that bring all existence together in unity.

On another occasion, I showed this student an onion and asked him whether he regarded it as a single entity or not. He replied that he did because the onion appeared to ''be all connected together.'' I then had him examine the onion under a microscope, and, as I had expected, he was nonplused by what he saw. Magnified only a hundred times, an onion, far from seeming to ''be all connected together,'' becomes a mass of independent cells, each struggling valiantly to preserve its own identity and some displaying a turbulent flow of liquid within them.

If a person is trained to see things the way a microscope does, I suppose he must see everything as pluralistic. I imagine that Dr. Hideki Yukawa, who won a Nobel Prize for his research on intermediate particles, and Dr. Reona Ezaki, who received the same award for his study of tunnels in semiconductors, must even see water as a collection of separate molecules. That view, however, is for specialists.

Look at it from a different angle. Suppose you were on the American Jupiter probe, Pioneer 10, attempting to take pictures of the earth from the vicinity of Jupiter. To your unaided eye, the earth would look a great deal smaller than an onion (think how Jupiter, which is much larger than the earth, looks to us), and it would have to be enlarged thousands of times for you to be able to make out people or machines.

But this must be the way that the eye of the all-seeing Buddha sees our planet. Though we, with our smaller view, see ourselves as separate individuals with individual bodies, individual wills, individual thoughts, individual talents, individual lives, and so on, the eye of the Buddha sees all existence as forming one great cosmos, in which the movements of universal life cause a continual panorama of sadness and joy, laughter and tears, harmony and discord.

It could be that the Buddha alone is the active force moving this universe and that we are only passive beings shifting about under his control. If this were the case, we could say that we were, not living, but being caused to live. Young people do not take very kindly to this view. If we are all controlled by some higher power, they argue, then we are no more than automatons, and life itself is meaningless.

Young people in particular, it would seem, consider passivity to be retrogressive and shameful. I, for my share, think that young people who have the courage to live in a period such as our own ought to be able to recognize the value of being passive (being able to be passive) when passivity is what is needed.

I believe that the world today is going through a great crisis. While wondering how we can manage to live through it, I worry lest I merely add to the general uncertainty by calling attention to our plight.

There are times, I think, when one must move as energetically as one possibly can—full speed ahead, as it were. But in an age when we can clearly see the limits of the world's natural resources, I do not see how we can afford not to try to adjust ourselves to the will of nature and the disposition of heaven. At the risk of appearing overly dramatic, I must say that I see absolutely no other way for mankind to survive. In our contemporary context, it seems to me that we need more people who know how to be passive, for such people harmonize both with other people and with machines, thus acquiring the true active nature that enables them to use both men and machines with consummate skill.

I am thinking, for instance, of a wise wife, who seems to heed her husband's every wish but is able in doing so to evoke all his hidden strength and talent for leadership.

One very cold winter I went skiing with a group of young people. I was not completely inexperienced, but the first time we went out on the mountainside I kept falling down.

"Your legs are too tight, sir," advised one of the boys. "Your knees need to be looser, so they can bend with the ups and downs." I tried cushioning myself with my knees and managed to get over one hump very nicely, but on the next one I fell on my rear again.

I sat there for a while watching the younger people ski past on a steep and bumpy slope. It was marvelous how flexible their bodies were. Their knees were bending and unbending continually, but the upper parts of their bodies were moving along at the same level, as though they were sliding down a perfectly smooth course. I realized then that the truth of truths for skiers is a passive stance in which the legs bend or stretch in response to the terrain. The course is a continuous series of ups and downs —when you've negotiated one you must be ready for the next immediately. Only when a person has acquired what I now call "passive knees" can he ski with reasonable skill and safety. It seems to me that the secret for getting through the crisis our civilization now faces is much the same. We must develop a flexibility of spirit in which active is identical with passive and passive is identical with active.

One of the most famous sections of the Lotus Sutra is the parable of the burning house. A father, hearing that his house is on fire, rushes home and calls to his children to get out of the burning building. The children are so busy playing, however, that they do not notice the danger. There is not enough time for the father to run in and rescue them; the only hope is that they will see the light and come out on their own. To entice them, the father cries, "If you come outside, I'll give you splendid new toys!" Attracted by the idea of the gifts, the children all run outside. Only then do they see that they have been in danger of being burned to death.

The children are ourselves, fretting and beating our breasts over the sad state of contemporary civilization. The father attempting to save us is the Buddha. He sees through us and perceives that what we must each do is use the strength that is in him to jump free of the flames. But too many of us are busy asking how the strength of one person or even of two or three persons can save the whole of society. We do not hear.

In fact, the strength that each of us has within our grasp is phenomenal if we only know how to use it properly.

If I asked you whether you could start or stop a truck with a single thread, you would laugh. But you *can* start or stop a truck with a single string if the string is attached to a switch that operates the truck's accelerator and brake.

A similar method can be used to give society a push in the right direction. Each person who belongs to this society has within him a motivating force that functions like the engine of a truck. If you can control this force and move it in the proper direction, society will go right along with it. The fact that the husbands of this world are able to influence their wives has nothing to do with brute strength; wives are guided by their desire to go along with their husbands, whom they love.

The Buddha is trying to control us in such a way as to enable us to lead peaceful, abundant lives. To ignore this and instead to fly off the handle because of some short-range problem that faces us is tantamount to pulling the string too hard and making the truck go too fast. When this is done, the truck is likely to run over somebody.

On the other hand, when the Buddha loosens the reins, we must not blindly decide that there is no future; we must not put ourselves into reverse so that nothing can move us forward, for that is as dangerous as going forward too rapidly.

In the end, what we must remember is that the active and passive principles are interdependent. Either one is dangerous without the other, but in balance they can bring peace and happiness to the world.

IO

A Heartbeat That Has Lasted
a Hundred Million Years

We all seem to be convinced that we know a great deal about the world we live in. When we see something or hear something, we feel certain that we recognize its significance, and this confidence in our own knowledge enables us to live from day to day without too much worry.

But from time to time I stop and ask myself just how much we really know about the world. I am confident that I am alive and moving, here and at this moment. But what is it that enables me to move? . . .

We appear to have all sorts of information, but I can't help feeling that the average person is only managing somehow to get by, without knowing the essential facts of life. When the society around us runs smoothly and harmoniously, we take its movements for granted and make no great effort to find out what makes it tick. But when something gets out of whack and things begin to go wrong, we suddenly find ourselves compelled to think about basics, because the common sense by which we set such store is not enough to carry us through.

Once a few years ago a lathe in my laboratory went on the

blink. In case you're not quite sure what a lathe is, it's a machine that scrapes and files metal rods until they are perfectly round. It can also ream out round metal blocks to make cylinders, put the threads on screws, and do numerous other tooling operations. The lathe is a basic machine for making parts that go into other machines.

When a piece of metal is processed on a lathe, the lathe causes it to spin rapidly, and the operator employs a blade, called a bit, to chisel the whirling metal until it is perfectly round. In order for this to happen, the metal itself must be turning in a perfect circle, which means that the shaft, or spindle, of the lathe must also be perfectly cylindrical.

When our lathe broke, it happened that I was in too much of a hurry for a particular rod to wait until the machine could be fixed. I therefore had to try to shape the rod with an ordinary file. As I did so, I remembered an incident that had occurred years earlier, when I was a student.

I had been working with a lathe then, too, and I suddenly began to wonder how the spindle, which had to be perfectly round, was made. I asked my teacher, and he burst into laughter. "You mean the round shaft that's used on your lathe?" he asked, to make sure. I nodded. "Why, that," he continued, still grinning, "was made on a lathe that existed before yours did."

In that case, how was the spindle on the older lathe made? You guessed it: on a still older lathe. And the spindle on that? . . . To make a long story short, my desire to know how the first perfectly round spindle came into existence quickly took me back to the year 1797, when an English mechanic named Henry Maudslay (1771–1831) devised an automatic lathe. But even that was not the end of the story, because the spindle Maudslay used had probably been made on an earlier hand-turned lathe—and the spindle on that, on an even more primitive device that could only carve perfect circles.

In other words, the lathe in my laboratory, turning out a perfectly cylindrical rod, was started up centuries ago by someone somewhere who had succeeded in making a perfectly cylindrical spindle or shaft.

To explain why I myself am moving here and now requires the same sort of historical questioning. I know that if my heart stopped beating, I would cease to live, but how does it come about that my heart is beating in the first place?

When I first took up residence in my mother's womb, I did not even have a heart, let alone a heartbeat. But as the cells split and formed the embryo of a baby, blood vessels came into being, and gradually a faint pulsation began. Part of the blood system took the form of the heart, which became the center of the beating. But the actual origin of the heartbeat has a hereditary connection with the mother and father, and through them with all earlier direct ancestors. From there it goes back to primitive man, then to some form of monkey, and eventually to the amoeba, which is a basic form of life. My heartbeat, then, was started hundreds of millions of years ago in the pulsations of an amorphous speck of protoplasm.

All this may sound far-fetched to some people, but it is nonetheless true. Actually, there were already mammals on our planet a hundred million years ago, and the process of successive reproduction whereby the human race evolved was well under way. If at any point along the way the heartbeat in a given lineage had stopped, that lineage would have come to an end. Perhaps you or I might never have been born. From the time when the heart of the fetus begins to beat until the child is safely born, the mother's heart must continue to beat.

But my purpose in bringing this subject up was not to go on at length about the human heart. What I wished to do was call your attention to the power and the flow of nature's life-force. The heart, to be sure, is a convenient example, because in some ways it is virtually synonymous with life.

The spark of life that lives in you and me today did not begin with our mammalian ancestors of a hundred million years back or even with the amoeba, which came into existence several hundred million years earlier. The fact is that even the amoeba had ancestors. But when we go back this far, we are in an age when life in the ordinary sense did not exist. What we find instead is inorganic matter—the atoms of basic elements like carbon, hydrogen, and sodium. Still earlier, there must have been protons, electrons, neutrons, and mesons; and I am told that in the more advanced ranks of physics, scholars are studying even more elemental forms of matter or energy.

In any case, as I consider the whole process of evolution, I am impressed by the following four points:

1. There is a basic life-force that forms and moves everything from the elementary particle through the atom, the molecule, inorganic matter, organic matter, complex molecules, unicellular life, multicellular life, human beings, society, and the world to the entire cosmos. In Buddhism, this life-force is called *kū* (in Japanese), or *śūnyatā* (in Sanskrit), or the Void.

2. This life-force has been in existence eternally; our own lives are of course the result of its workings.

3. Life is not limited to what is usually called organic matter, but is also found in inorganic matter. (Actually, scientists who have studied the problem in depth say that there is no distinct line between organic and inorganic matter.) In other words, not only animals and people, but minerals as well, have life.

4. Man must number among his ancestors not only father and mother, grandfathers and grandmothers, great-grandfathers and great-grandmothers, but also all earlier forms from which he is descended, including monkeylike hominids, amoebas, inorganic atoms, and elementary particles.

Looked at in this fashion, our life is not a brief event that begins when our mothers bear us and ends when we die. Instead, it is identical with the cosmic life that from the eternal past to the eternal future manifests the fundamental life-force, or *kū*.

The great life of the cosmos is never-ceasing. Each breath we take, each beat of our hearts, is a part of this unending movement. Before all else, we must awaken ourselves to the cosmic life within us. Otherwise, we cannot begin to know the world we live in as it really exists.

There are, in brief, entirely too many important things that most people never notice. The world works, generators whirl, lathes and motors spin, there is action everywhere, but no one pays any attention to the ubiquitous life-force that causes everything, including ourselves, to move.

Nearly twenty years ago the Japanese building code was altered in such a way as to make it permissible for the first time to construct buildings higher than 31 meters. The first important structure to go up in Tokyo under the new regulations was the Kasumigaseki Building, which, although only 36 stories high, became a symbol of the skyscraper in Japan.

By way of startling my university students into taking a closer look at the world around them, not long after the Kasumigaseki Building was completed, I assigned as the theme for a term paper a comparison between the new skyscraper and a long-stemmed carnation. When I announced the subject, the class eyed me suspiciously, as I had expected them to, and I proceeded to explain.

"I'm not pulling your leg," I said, "nor am I assigning you an impossible topic. Everything that exists is related to everything else. I want you to discover the truth of this for yourselves, and that is why I have asked you to compare two things that you probably now think of as entirely different."

What I expected the students to do was start with a height comparison. On the face of it, of course, there *is* no comparison because the Kasumigaseki Building rises about 140 meters above the ground while the carnation grows to a height of no more than 30 centimeters. This very discrepancy, however, ought to lead a student with an inquiring mind to ask just what height is. Is it a matter of so many meters off the ground, or is it something more? A student would soon come to the conclusion, I think, that height is most meaningful if thought of in connection with breadth. If we are comparing a building to the stem of a flower, the relevant point is the relative value of the vertical rise with respect to the horizontal spread. If we consider this aspect, the carnation is much taller than the Kasumigaseki Building.

Before the revision of the building code, tall buildings were required to have rigid-frame structures, which were considered to be safe against earthquakes. In the 1950s, however, it became the majority view among architects that flexible structures were in fact safer, because the shaking of their parts during an earthquake effectively absorbs the shock without causing the building to collapse. To a large extent, this consideration caused the removal of the Japanese height limitation, and the Kasumigaseki Building is, as we would expect, a flexible-frame structure.

Actually, architects say that the real danger in high-rise buildings is not from earthquakes but from the wind. During a typhoon, the force of the wind a hundred meters up is ferocious. No doubt the Kasumigaseki Building has been designed to withstand winds with a wallop greater than has ever been experienced in Japan, but one suspects that the carnation is even stronger in this respect. Despite the top-heaviness caused by its large blossom, the carnation is very rarely blown down by the wind, no matter how it might sway. Concealed in the structure of its stem, leaves, and flowers are the subtlest principles of structural dynamics.

What is to be gained from looking at commonplace things from a different angle? In my opinion, we can neither form an accurate view of society nor assume our proper role in it unless we think of things and see them from various different angles, not just two. Without extreme care, human beings nearly always view every object, every person, and every event from one direction only; normally, we think of these things in only one way and understand only one aspect of anything we consider (if indeed one aspect can be said to be "understood" apart from other aspects). No matter how thoroughly we believe we have studied a subject, there is always an opposing view from the other side.

Look at something from behind, from above, from below, from the side—how it looks depends entirely on where you are looking from. Yet one of the pitfalls we stumble over most frequently is that of assuming that the side we have seen first is the only side that exists. The only way to learn to get at the essence of things is to form the habit of looking at everything from more than one viewpoint. If at first you see no other viewpoint than your own, look around a bit, and you will find it. It always exists.

At the risk of offending nonsmokers, I confess that I smoke fifteen or sixteen cigarettes a day and, for reasons suggested elsewhere, have no great qualms about this. About the only conscious thoughts I ever have about cigarettes are, "My, this tastes good!" and "My throat's dry—must have smoked too many today."

Let me now try to think of cigarettes in a completely different way from any in which I have ever thought of them before. Let's see . . . an idea is forming. I think I've got it—a leading question.

Who was the first person who ever conceived of *smoking* tobacco leaves? When you consider it, wasn't that a truly remarkable idea? Tobacco is a leafy plant, like cabbage or spinach or lettuce. Almost anyone might think of cutting the leaves and serving them with mayonnaise. But how did anyone figure out in his head that people (certain people, at any rate) could derive pleasure from rolling up a tobacco leaf, setting fire to one end of it, and inhaling the smoke from the other? Whether you approve of smoking or not, you must admit that the conception is ingenious. Furthermore, the idea of shredding the leaf and wrapping just enough for one smoke in a piece of thin paper is almost equally ingenious. This must surely have been the origin of unit packaging, which has become a commercial and industrial vogue in the past decade or two.

I cannot refrain from observing that when a tobacco leaf is cut up and put into a cigarette, its fate is diversified in an unusual way. About a third of the cigarette it goes into will have the original function of being smoked. The middle third will serve as a filter at first and be smoked later, but the remaining third, after serving as a filter, will probably be thrown away and crushed underfoot, without ever having served the purpose for which it was grown. Still, the life of the last third is not completely useless, because if it were not there no one would be able to smoke the first two thirds.

With a little effort, as you see, I can find numerous thoughts to think about cigarettes that I have never thought before. You will find, if you look about you, that almost everything lends itself to being viewed in more ways than one. When you have tried looking at your fountain pen, your watch, and other possessions in various different ways, the next step is to consider your family, your friends, your fellow workers, and the events that occur in the world about you. You will be amazed at how different things are from what you thought. You will also be amazed at how much you learn from the most ordinary objects when you take the trouble to consider them from numerous viewpoints.

II

Proving the Equation X = X′

The fundamental ideal in the Buddha's teachings is the Middle
Path, which is to say a view of life and a way of living that veer
toward no extreme. We may begin to approach the Middle Path,
it seems to me, by viewing everything and thinking of everything
from all possible viewpoints.

This is not, let us observe, the manner of traditional scholar-
ship, which tends to divide things and to emphasize their differences. In the traditional fashion, we say, for example, "This is
not an orange, an apple, or a persimmon, so it must be a pear."
Thought processes of this sort become a habit, and before long we
have formed rules, such as:

> What is not beautiful is ugly.
> What is not right is wrong.
> What is not good is evil.

In other words, we tend more and more to divide things into
two opposing categories. When we do this, the longer we study,
the more we become prisoners of straight-line, single-aspect,
either-or thinking.

117

But in fact the world does not divide itself neatly into black and white. What has a front has a back; what has a right has a left; what has a top has a bottom. So long as we see only one of many aspects, no matter how thoroughly we examine that aspect, we cannot know the true form of the object as a whole.

The best proof of this is that if one person or one group looks at something in one way, it is only a matter of time before there appears another person or group who looks at it in a diametrically opposite way. People who see things only from the right side give birth to people who see things only from the left side. When someone describes the beauties of the view from above, wait around a while and someone else will tell you how seamy it all looks from below. It is a fact of life that a single-aspect view invariably evokes an opposite-aspect view. So long as both remain uncompromising, the conflict between them can only grow sharper and more violent. What is the end result? A world divided into east and west; nations divided into north and south; national assemblies divided into left and right; labor and management always at each other's throats; students mauling other students over whether they belong to the correct revolutionary party or not. It is in the face of all this that the Buddha says, "Do not divide and cause conflicts. Find a way to bring everything together." And as a means for viewing the true oneness of the cosmos, which is ultimate reality, the Buddha has given us the following mathematical equation:

$$X = X' \text{ (}X' \text{ being anything opposite to X).}$$

In other words, opposites are to be viewed as identical. One may fill in the unknown quantities as follows:

$$\text{Sacred} = \text{Not sacred.}$$

The person whose viewpoint and way of thinking are rigidly fixed cannot believe this. He will not understand why the Buddha saw the purest of purities within the sullied and the vulgar; why he considered sacred and profane to be essentially the same. These loftier concepts become available only as one casts away predetermined concepts and adopts a multifaceted approach.

Since I suspect that some readers are inclined to disagree with me, I shall labor my point a bit further.

In school, at home, in society, there are always parents, teachers, and superiors who tell us, "Don't act that way, act this way." And among the persons so admonished, there are always some who react adversely. If told they must go east, not west, they almost automatically determine that they will go west. When I come up against a student of this type, I say, "All right then, go west if you wish, but don't stop halfway. Make a thorough job of it."

Luckily the world is round. If the student goes west from Japan, past China to Europe, past Europe to America, across America, he will arrive in California, which is where he would probably be if he'd gone east as advised. He will have suffered no great loss by being contrary, though this is not necessarily true in all cases.

I feel sure you have all listened any number of times to a symphony orchestra, and I therefore assume that you will quickly understand why I regard a symphony orchestra as an example of the Buddhist teaching that "one is all and all is one." In a typical symphonic composition, there will be places where only part of the orchestra is playing and other places where all of the instruments are playing. In the latter places, called *tutti* (the Italian for all), the total sound is heard all at once, but if you listen carefully you can pick out the sound of the flutes or the violas or whichever instruments you wish to hear. When you stop making an effort to hear particular parts, the whole comes through again as before. The curious fact is that this phenomenon—being able to hear either the whole or the parts—is most pronounced when you are listening to a first-rate orchestra like the Berlin Philharmonic, which plays together perfectly. When you listen to an orchestra that has not practiced enough and is therefore out of step, you will find difficulty hearing either the whole or the parts. A good orchestra seems to me a perfect illustration of oneness in diversity and diversity in oneness.

I used to work in a research institute that had 700 members. This being a large organization, there were five administrative divisions, separated as it happened by scholarly discipline. The first division was physics; the second, machinery; the third, electricity; the fourth, applied science; and the fifth, architecture and civil engineering. As time went on, there were more and more projects involving two or more divisions simultaneously, and the people in charge began to feel that three divisions would be more efficient than five. But because of personal feelings, it proved difficult to reduce five divisions to three. Essentially, the problem was that two persons would have to give up the prestigious position of division chief, and it was difficult to decide which two.

As we considered possible solutions, I said, "Instead of decreasing the number of divisions, why not increase it?"

"*Increase* it?"

"Yes, you can increase it right out of existence."

"What are you talking about? How many divisions do you have in mind?"

"Seven hundred, or the exact number of members we have. That way everybody would be a division chief. We would appear to have lots and lots of divisions, but in fact we would have none."

Everyone admitted that there was something to be said for the idea, because it took positive advantage of the contemporary tendency of groups to split into smaller and smaller units. My seven-hundred-section organization would have been another example of "all is one," I think. Perhaps the type of thinking employed here might help to explain the Buddhist teaching that he who has nothing has everything (in other words, zero equals infinity).

From the above three illustrations, I think it ought to be clear that the equation $X = X'$ is by no means nonsense. Let us therefore pursue the idea a little farther.

I imagine that many of you believe, as I once believed, that things can be classified as good or bad. People must think this, because in everyday conversation they are always saying, "Oh, that's perfect," or "No, that's no good." In a general way, of course, it is essential that we all have a sense of what is good and what is bad, but if we are not careful we apply these labels to things before we have really thought the matter over. Carried too far, this tendency can lead us into the fallacy of assuming that good and evil are objective attributes of existence—that certain things are intrinsically good or evil. We might then come to believe, for example, that tape recorders are good, whereas bombs are bad.

Tape recorders *are* good, of course. They make it possible for us to soothe our spirits with beautiful music whenever we wish, or to record outstanding performances and replay them as often as we choose. But tape recorders are also bad, because they make it easy for wicked people to record secret conversations and make unscrupulous use of them later. Bombs, for their part, are bad when they are used destructively, as they usually are; but they can be good when they are used to facilitate mining or tunnel construction.

Anyone can see from this that the choice between good and bad is not necessarily simple. In fact, it can be even more difficult than so far suggested. Recording beautiful music and playing it back is a pleasant experience, but a person who gets used to hearing only beautiful music becomes highly vulnerable to ordinary noise. He may find himself unable to survive in the usual urban surroundings, and this in itself is not very good.

By pointing out how a good thing can become a bad thing or a bad thing good, I am not trying to confuse you. I simply hope you

OBJECT	GOOD ASPECTS OR USES	BAD ASPECTS OR USES
Fire	Cooking, sterilization	Difficult to control, dangerous
Water	Quenching thirst, washing	Causes floods, drowning
Blade	Serves as scalpel	Serves as switchblade
Bacterial activity	Fermentation	Decomposition, spoilage
Automobile	Serves as ambulance	Kills people on road
Atomic energy	Energy of the future	Source of atomic bombs
Hands	Used for nearly all work	Used for murder and other crimes
Mouth	Communication	Source of trouble
Waste	Recoverable resource	Garbage
Sense of justice	Cause of peace	Cause of war
Truth	Source of happiness	Source of unhappiness

will see that everything has both a good and a bad aspect. A list of examples is given in the table above, which I hope you will look at carefully. As is indicated there, fire and water are needed to make life livable, but either a conflagration or a flood can endanger many human lives. Atomic energy, the force employed in atomic bombs, is the most fearful explosive hitherto employed by mankind, but we may well have to depend upon it as a source of energy once we have exhausted our supply of petroleum.

If you find difficulty in seeing what I mean, it is probably because you are so busy thinking about things outside you (objective being) that you have not yet become aware of the workings of your own mind. The truth is that what is outside you is neither good nor bad, but neutral. It merely exists, but since we look upon it with feelings based on desire—since, in other words, we either like or dislike it—it becomes divided in our sight into good and bad. The best examples are fermentation and decomposition. Both of these are caused by the activities of bacteria. When the resulting product is bread or wine or something else that people use and like, we call the bacterial activity fermentation; but when the end product is a smelly, poisonous substance, we call it decomposition or spoilage.

If we take a second look at the garbage in our dump heaps and devise ways of utilizing it, it becomes a valuable resource; if we ignore its potentialities, it remains what it is—waste. But, as you can see from this one example, the fundamental cause of good or bad is not within the object outside ourselves, but within our own minds. This point is of the utmost importance.

Take the case of the scalpel and the switchblade, which I noted earlier in a similar context. Both have cutting edges ten-odd centimeters long; both are intended to slice human flesh; both are neutral as far as good or evil is concerned. But as soon as human feelings are involved, the scalpel becomes good while the switchblade becomes bad. The scalpel is good because it is used with the spirit of the Buddha, which seeks to save men; the switchblade is bad because it is used with the spirit of the devil, which seeks to kill men. Dependent on the heart of the user, the same cutting edge may be either of two opposite extremes.

No one doubts the importance of a sense of justice, but even a sense of justice can cause serious problems. Today wars are going on in several parts of the world, and the fundamental reason for each of them is a conflict of opinions as to what is right and what is wrong. Each party to each battle will assure you, usually in tones of righteous indignation, that its cause is just—that it is the opposing side that seeks to impose injustice. Like the blade that can cure or kill, the uses of a sense of justice are dependent upon the hearts of the users.

What the above discussion boils down to, as you no doubt realize by now, is that:

$$Good = Bad\ (\ = Neither)$$

$$or \quad X = X'.$$

The table on page 121 indicates that everything has both a good and a bad aspect. The implication is that no matter how sure we are that we are engaged in a good and worthy activity, we must constantly be on guard against possible evil effects.

About fifteen years ago, the people of Japan, fired by dreams of doubling their personal incomes within a decade, pitched in and carried through a remarkable nationwide campaign for economic growth. We all hoped that the Japanese economy would expand rapidly, that wages would soar, and that everyone would become affluent. We genuinely believed that these goals and our efforts to achieve them were good.

But things did not turn out quite as we expected. Before long there arose problems: pollution, political corruption, personal alienation or disorientation. From this one experience, in which nearly all Japanese participated to some extent, it should be clear that the minute we accept something as absolutely good, we cease to take adequate precautions against evil, with the result that it soon steals its way into the scene.

If that's the case, some may say, how can we put ourselves wholeheartedly into any work we regard as good? How can we be sure it is actually good? How can we accomplish anything good if we're constantly afraid we might be doing something bad?

These questions are understandable, but there is indeed a way. To find it we need go only a step farther.

The difference between good and bad is, as I have said, in the heart. If the heart is in proper condition, a dangerous knife becomes a life-saving instrument rather than a murderous weapon. But to talk about the heart being in proper condition is one thing, and, for most people, to make sure it actually is, is quite another. One tries to think good, but evil little thoughts are always lurking about in the shadows of one's mind: "If nobody knows about it, a little slip here and there doesn't matter" or "I may as well help myself to a little before the others arrive." If we have not disciplined ourselves long and ardently, little temptations like these are bound to assert themselves. Such being the case, we often convince ourselves that we are doing the right thing only to discover along the way that something has gone wrong, that we have unwittingly used the switchblade rather than the scalpel.

The essential point is that the heart must be in the proper condition—or, as we say colloquially, in the right place. If your heart is not amiss, you can put yourself wholeheartedly behind any good cause, confident that you will not inadvertently bring harm to someone. When your heart is right, you don't bring out the bad side of things—only the good side emerges. But first you must make sure your heart is functioning as it ought to.

If you own a car, you no doubt send it to the garage for periodic checkups. Even on ordinary days, you watch it yourself to make sure that the brakes are not loose or the engine missing. You give your body similar attention. If you have a sore throat or a fever or a backache, you go to a doctor and maybe take a day or two off until you're better.

Why is it that people take pretty good care of their cars and their bodies, but ignore the condition of their hearts, which is far more important? Most of us don't even seem to recognize the need for a regular checkup in this area. Yet the heart is an infinitely more complicated mechanism than an automobile—one that is more difficult to drive and at the same time more susceptible to breakdowns if not cared for assiduously.

As a designer and builder of robots, I am constantly reminded that the heart, which is to say the apparatus with which we think and feel, must be kept under constant surveillance, for its mechanism is the most intricate and delicate of all. Tending robots has taught me many lessons about the human heart, and over the years I have composed a checklist for determining whether your heart is in tiptop shape or not. In the hope that it will help you develop a clean and beautiful heart, I offer it here:

1. There should be no ego. You should feel yourself to be united with everything around you. This condition constitutes selflessness and accords with the Buddhist principle that "nothing has an ego."

2. You are not attempting to better your own position, but instead are trying to benefit others. You wish to help even those who regard you as an enemy. Your own needs do not seem important to you. You are full of gratitude to the entire external world—including tools and machines as well as people—for making it possible for you to live. You are full of vitality and long to live a worthwhile life.

3. There is nothing rough or violent about your mental state. You feel love and compassion not only for all living beings, but also for inanimate objects as well.

4. Since you know that you are alive because of the force of *kū*, or *śūnyatā* (the Void), which is the great life-force of the cosmos, there is nothing that can anger you. You are not upset when others speak ill of you.

5. You are envious of no one. You rejoice in the beauty and success of others as though they were your own.

6. You are modest, not given to vanity, and law-abiding. You can regard anything or anybody as your teacher, whether it be plant or mineral, of higher station or lower.

7. Not only are you not stingy with goods and money (hardware); you are equally generous in sharing information and knowledge (software) with others. You know the significance of the existence of all things and are able to make use of them. At the same time, you are careful to save, rather than waste.

8. Things do not exercise a hold on you. You are able to part with your most prized possession if necessary.

9. You like to exert yourself and have no inclination to be lazy. You are able to enjoy hard work.

10. Your brain is being used to the full, and wisdom flows from it as water from a spring. You see things accurately, and not as though through a cloud.

I hardly need say that none of us arrives very quickly or easily at the sublime state I have outlined. But merely to try to condition your heart in the fashion prescribed here is an exhilarating experience. Anyone who likes to tinker with mechanical devices knows that, alongside the pleasure of operating a perfectly tuned machine, there is an almost equal joy in trying to repair a damaged machine so that it will run like new. The same is true of your heart.

When the heart is in perfect condition by the standards listed above, it has entered the state of enlightenment. In Zen Buddhism there is a series of ten pictures showing the process whereby an ordinary mortal looks for and finds the enlightenment of the Buddha.

The Buddha is represented in the paintings as an ox. In the first picture, the supplicant, having asked many people where he can find the Buddha, and having concluded that the Buddha is in the mountains, begins walking in the direction of the mountains. In the next picture, the supplicant sees the ox's footprints and knows he is on the right trail. The third picture shows the supplicant as he spies the rear end of the ox and catches hold of its tail. In the fourth picture, the supplicant has thrown a net over the ox, but is having difficulty managing the animal. The meaning here is that the supplicant has not really achieved buddhahood, but is not fully aware of this fact. In the fifth picture, the ox is beginning to act as the supplicant wishes, which means that the supplicant's own actions now accord with the Law, though he has not yet attained to buddhahood.

The sixth picture shows the supplicant on his way back home, mounted on the ox. He has discovered that the Buddha is to be found not in remote places, but in the everyday world. Happy because he has now learned to live in accordance with the Law, he joyfully plays a flute. The ox is not seen in the seventh picture, because the supplicant's mind and body now move in accord with the Law even though he is not consciously seeking the Buddha.

In the eighth picture, the supplicant has also disappeared, the significance being that he has now fused with the unseeable Buddha. Even this, however, does not mean that he has entered the ultimate state of enlightenment. In the ninth picture, we see the origin of existence, in which the willow is green, the flowers are red, blossoms bloom in spring, and leaves fall in autumn. Finally, in the tenth picture, the supplicant has lost his wish to be this or that and is content with what he is. He is in the land of the completely natural and flawless, where if he is happy he laughs, if he is cold he shivers, if he is hungry he eats. He is no longer imprisoned by desire, nor does he go beyond the limits of the Law. This perfectly natural state is the sphere of the Buddha's final enlightenment. From outward appearances, the supplicant is no different from when he started out. He was in the form of the Buddha from the beginning, had he only had the enlightenment to see it.

But if all that is necessary is to do as he pleases, why couldn't he simply have done as he pleased from the first and saved himself a lot of bother? Because ordinary people, despite what they think, are not able to live as they please. They can start doing so, but they cannot keep it up very long, because they lack the restraint of the Law and are governed by desire. They eat everything they want and think how fortunate they are to be able to do so, but, since they do not know how to stop, presently they find themselves in agony from overeating. Whatever they do, they do to excess, because they are moved by longing, rather than by the contentment of enlightenment.

The enlightened man knows how to restrain all his desires and wishes, while at the same time behaving in a perfectly natural way. It is to achieve this happy state that we must condition our hearts. It is for this that the Buddhist discipline exists.

12

Having Eyes to See

We all have two eyes, and nearly all of us have great faith in our eyes. We say, ''It happened just this way—I saw it with my own two eyes.'' Or, oppositely, ''That couldn't be true—I was standing here with my eyes wide open and I didn't see anything of the sort.'' You have all heard statements like this countless times. Their underlying meaning is that people have a strong tendency to accept as absolute truth that which they themselves have seen, heard, or felt. By the same token, they resent being asked to understand or believe in things they cannot see, hear, or touch. In such matters, they set their own sensory perception up as an absolute criterion. What is more, they seem to think this is the empiric, or scientific, approach to life. Scientists I know, however, including myself, are more and more hesitant, the more they study science, to accept their own judgment as final. In fact, it has been my observation that the study of science tends to demonstrate our weakness most clearly on those occasions when we insist upon the validity of our own experience. In that respect, science resembles the teachings of the Buddha.

The world today is full of people studying various subjects and becoming absorbed in various kinds of work. I think it no exaggeration to say that all this study, all this work, is ultimately in pursuit of the Buddha's enlightenment. People who study economics and become economic experts, people who study literature or music or painting, people who are trying to find ways of making their housework more efficient . . . all those who are going diligently about their study or their chores are, in my opinion, learning one by one the teachings of the Buddha and by so doing are gradually acquiring the truth that the Buddha arrived at. All too few of us recognize this, however.

For that reason, I have chosen to take science, which is my specialty, as an example and to show how closely the learning of scientific facts is related to the Buddha's teachings. What I say in the following pages about science may be regarded as being about Buddhism. If you read it with this in mind, I believe you will discover clues to the connection between your own field of endeavor and the ultimate truth of Buddhism. At least, I hope you will find them.

First, let us consider the phenomenon of seeing.

Fifteen or twenty years ago, Japanese scientists and engineers specializing in automation were constantly organizing "inspection groups" to travel to the United States and see the results of factory automation there. America was at that time the model for the rest of the world in this field. It was *the* place to study.

As a rule, Japanese experts arriving in the United States were taken aback by the bigness of everything. They wrote of enormous plains with fields of soybeans stretching in all directions "as far as the eye could see" and of perfectly straight highways extending down through the fields apparently to infinity. When taken to factories, they inspected the automated facilities down to the last bolt and screw, then wrote reports that went like this: "The automated processes at such-and-such a plant in the state of such-and-such is run by IBM Model 0000 computers and has a capacity of. . . ."

I had read any number of similar reports and been duly impressed before I was asked by a Japanese producer of soybean oil to join an inspection tour of America. The producer wanted me to take a look and then advise him on the automation of his own plant.

The first thing that impressed me in the United States was not the factory but the soybeans themselves. A popular name for young soybeans in Japan is "twig beans," because they grow on short twigs extending from the stalks. Bunches of "twig beans," boiled and salted, are served as tidbits with beer or sakè. The name "twig beans" hardly prepared me for the soybeans I saw in America, which were attached directly to the stalk. "Stalk beans," I thought, "not twig beans."

Investigation revealed that these soybeans were an improved breed developed to facilitate automation. In order to harvest ordinary "twig beans," the beans must be picked, twigs and all, by a tractor and then separated from the twigs and hulled by a different machine. In other words, two distinct operations are required. When soybeans are raised on as large a scale as they are in the United States, the cost of two separate operations is very great—great enough to cause farmers (agribusinessmen) to change the beans themselves to permit one-operation harvesting.

I groaned at the sight of these "improved" beans. As it happens, the first step in mechanizing work hitherto done by human beings is to redesign the processes so that they lend themselves to automation. This is basic, and the conversion of "twig beans" to "stalk beans" must have been the prerequisite for the automation program that developed. All of my Japanese predecessors had seen the beans, but not one of them had paid any attention to them. So busy had they been looking at machinery that they failed to notice the change in the raw product that made the whole apparatus feasible. This is what is known as not having the eyes to see. To the unseeing eye, truth is invisible.

We use the word "see" in many ways. At times to see is merely a passive operation in which something appears before one but makes no impression. More often, to see implies consciousness of something visible. On a different level, to see can signify a purely mental operation, such as understanding or perceiving. Again, to see can mean to visualize, to imagine (create an image of), or to picture.

In Buddhist writings, "see" is very frequently used in the meaning of visualizing or understanding things that have no visible or tangible form. If one cannot see in this sense, one cannot achieve true enlightenment. To this, I must add that without this kind of vision one cannot become a genuine scientist or engineer either.

Let me give you an example of what I mean. A certain company once employed an engineer who was disturbed by the length of time it took carpenters to hammer a number of nails into place. The engineer began wondering if there were not some way to mechanize, and thereby expedite, this procedure. Asked to solve this problem, the average person would probably suggest putting a hammer in a robot's right hand and having the left hand hold the nails, which is what people ordinarily do. How to make a robot that would do this is not immediately apparent, but certainly it would not be impossible. The trouble is that in real life mechanization is not that simple. To make a machine perform exactly the same motions or operations as a human being can easily cost more than having a human being do them. In order to render mechanization feasible, it is usually necessary at about this stage to *see* something beyond, or perhaps within, what other people see. In this instance, while everyone else who attacked the problem was looking at the motions of the hands, our engineer began looking at the nails.

We automatically think of nails as coming in heaps or packages. We buy a handful or a sack of nails for so much, knowing that they will be all mixed up and will have to be taken out one by one for actual use. But the engineer I am speaking of suddenly "saw" a row of nails lined up neatly in a row like the staples used in a stapling machine. Once this vision had come to him, it was only a short step to visualizing an automatic nail-driver operated on the same principle as the Hotchkiss stapler. Instead of lying willy-nilly in a container, the nails are strung together neatly in rolls and placed in a cassette. The cassette is then attached to a pneumatic hammer that the carpenter operates by merely pulling a trigger.

To the scientific technician, vision is of paramount importance. The question is how to train the eye to see things that do not yet exist. We tend to take it for granted that vision is a matter of the strength of our eyes, but scientific studies show that this is an oversimplification.

How the United States Navy came to make an exhaustive study of the workings of frogs' eyes is an edifying story.

It all came about with the invention of that terrible device known as the guided missile. For a nation possessing guided missiles, it became possible two decades or so ago, to destroy cities halfway around the world simply by attaching nuclear warheads to the missiles. The American navy saw that New York or Washington could be reduced to cinders in a single stroke, and this was understandably disturbing to its leaders.

Was there no defense against the menace? Meetings were held, and it was pointed out that the best defense would be to intercept and destroy or divert missiles before they could reach American shores. Fine, but how? As great minds pondered the problem, an admiral suddenly stood up and said, "How would it be if we made a radar device that functions like a frog's eye?"

"A frog's eye?"

"Yes, a frog's eye. If you will observe, when an insect flying toward a frog comes within a certain range, the frog's tongue snaps out and ensnares it. How this is done is the secret of the frog's visual mechanism."

"Fantastic! When do we start?"

It is one of America's virtues that an oddball suggestion like this can be taken up and given the full treatment. Forthwith, billions of dollars were appropriated for research, and today we must know about all there is to know about the eyes of frogs.

At the back of the frog's eye is a reticular film. When light from without strikes this film, the light is converted into electric signals in a number proportional to the strength of the light. The signals are transmitted by four types of nerve fibers to the frog's brain. Each type of nerve fiber leads to a particular brain level. The first level reacts only to the outline of what is seen. The second responds only to images drawing closer to the center of the eye, which is to say, objects coming toward the frog. The third level reacts to variations in contrast, and so on. The net effect is that, although a great variety of images fall on the film in the back of the frog's eye, the frog sees only those that are approaching it and are more or less round—in other words, things, mostly insects, that are potential morsels of food. Objects standing still or moving away fall into the category of things that are invisible because the frog literally does not have the eye to see them.

The United States Navy's study of frogs' eyes has helped clarify the workings of the human eye as well. The human eye also has a light-receiving system: light is transmitted by a crystal-like lens to a reticulated film in the back of the eye, which converts it into electric impulses for transmission by nerves to the inner part of the brain. Only when these electric signals reach the inner brain do we actually see anything.

Seeing something in the brain is in essence distinguishing that something from other objects. Within the brain there are already "drawers" in which forms are classified as round or square, red or white, tall or short, and so on. By comparing the incoming image with the information in the "drawers"—an instantaneous operation—the brain determines whether it is "seeing" a white rice cake or a red apple.

Thanks to recent developments in the field of medicine, even people blind from birth because of defective corneas have been given a fair measure of vision by surgical transplants from the eye bank. A successful transplantation does not enable the patient to see as soon as he opens his eyes, however. At first, he can distinguish only the presence or absence of light. Not until his brain is equipped with the necessary memory "drawers" can he tell whether he is looking at a tea bowl or a tangerine or his mother's smiling face. The fact of the matter is, it is the brain that sees, not the eye.

Our eyes are many times as sophisticated as a frog's, but they, too, are more sensitive to moving objects than to stationary ones. When we look at objects standing still, our eyes move rapidly by way of compensation. I always thought that when I saw a beautiful woman my eyes took her in all at once, but new eye-testing devices reveal that this is not true. What actually happens is that I see the face, then the bust, then the hips, then the legs all in extremely rapid succession—too rapid for me to be conscious of more than one overall impression. A woman looking at another woman, by way of contrast, is likely to see first the hair (or the hairdo), then the clothes, then the rings before concluding that the woman she is looking at is not as stylish as she herself. When we read printed matter, our eyes oscillate at a frequency of about 100 times a second by way of creating motion where none exists.

We see clearly at one glance only a range corresponding to a visual angle of about 5°. Outside that limit, our power of vision drops quite drastically. We can see color only in the middle of our visual range, everything around the edges appearing in black and white (though we are not conscious of this). Although we think of ourselves as being able to see over a range of 180° or so, our eyes must move as far as possible from one side to the other to take all this in.

As with the eyes, so it is with the ears, the nose, and the fingers. What we see, hear, smell, and feel with is not the sensory organs, but the brain, particularly the cerebrum. In a broad sense, the meaning of this is that for each of us the entire world exists within an internal organ having a thickness of 2.5 millimeters and a total area of about 2,240 square centimeters. If this organ, the cerebrum, does not see or sense an object, neither does the object exist nor does it not exist for us. So long as the cerebrum feels nothing, we can know no such thing as pain.

The Buddha said that he was able to achieve enlightenment because he perceived that everything in the world exists through the law of cause and effect. Causes coincide with particular conditions to yield results of all kinds. In the process, things appear in visible form and then disappear as other things appear. Everything is always changing as causes and conditions mingle, giving rise to new causes and conditions. It is the Buddha's teaching that if we are able to discern the causes and conditions that produce everything in the world, we can gain true peace and tranquillity.

How does one discern this complex of causal factors? The Buddha's answer to this question is succinctly expressed in the term "right view." To acquire the "right view," which is the accurate and complete view, of things also happens to be the aim of those who specialize in science, though their field of investigation is more limited than the Buddha's. One important discovery scientists have already made is that the greatest hindrance to finding the "right view" is not a clouded lens, but a clouded mind.

Clouded mind? A mind that is hidden from reality by a veil of self-centered prejudices or preconceptions.

I once carried out a little experiment in which I asked a group of students from different fields of study to tell me what determines the thickness of electric wiring—in other words, what causes an engineer to choose one thickness as opposed to another for a particular job. I was not in the slightest surprised to find that the answers reflected the specialties of the answerers. Those in electrical engineering named the volume of the electric current as the governing factor. This is correct, because the thickness of the wire must be adjusted to the current. If the wire is too thin for the amperage, it will overheat.

Students in mechanical engineering, however, gave a different answer. According to them, the thickness depends on the tensile strength of the wire. This is true, too, because wires are frequently strung between poles and must be able to withstand the pull of gravity as well as a number of other forces. Even if the current to be carried is very small, a minimal thickness is necessary for mechanical reasons.

Students in management engineering came up with a third answer. For them, the determining factor is a list of building standards, which specifies wire thickness for various uses and situations. In actual fact, wire is sold only in standard gauges, and engineers do indeed employ tables for selecting the wire they will use.

All three answers were correct, so far as they went, but all were incorrect. Why incorrect? Because each answer took into consideration only one of the several functions an electric wire is called upon to perform.

It might be added that the man who "saw" all the functions of an electric wire was the inventor of the steel-core aluminum cable, which is now used for the high-voltage wiring you see hanging from steel towers throughout the countryside. The outer part of this wire, carrying the electric current, is made of aluminum, which is both light and cheap. The steel wire that forms the core provides the necessary tensile strength.

It is very easy to be misled by preconceptions. It happens to us all the time, particularly when we attempt to go by what we think of as common sense.

Do you happen to know why subway cars have windows even though they run back and forth in tunnels all the time? If you think it is so that people can see signs and advertisements posted in the subway stations, you are wrong. It's the other way around—the posters are there because the windows are. You would think the manufacturers of subway cars would find it simpler and cheaper to eliminate the windows, particularly since this would have the effect of strengthening the cars, yet for some reason the windows are there. Actually, one might conceive of numerous plausible explanations, but the truth is that there is nothing much to explain. It is just that when the first subways were built, they were equipped with trains that until that time had been running above ground.

Were you to be asked which hand of a watch—hour hand, minute hand, or second hand—is the least exact, you would probably say the hour hand. That stands to reason, because by looking at it alone we can determine the time only approximately. As it happens, however, the least precise of the three hands is the second hand, which most people look at not to pinpoint the time but to make sure the watch is running.

Preconceptions and fixed ideas will prevent you from seeing the truth each and every day of the week. This is particularly true in human relations. If you clothe yourself in a protective armor of self-concern, which makes you suspicious of other people's motives toward you, you are likely to misinterpret anything you see or hear.

To break free from the bonds of egoism and preconception is to open your eyes to the truth. If you practice the discipline of the "right view," you can rid yourself of blinding prejudices and gradually improve your total ability to see. When you come to know that the man walking down the opposite side of the street, the trains you ride on, the ants on the ground near your feet—in short, all things large or small—exist within your own mind, you will be ready to set aside your smaller, egoistic self and assume a grander self that is one with the eternal cosmos.

In his famous *Shōbō Genzō* (The Eye Storehouse of the True Law), the Zen master Dōgen (1200–1253) stated the case eloquently: "To learn the Way of the Buddha is to learn yourself. To learn yourself is to forget yourself."

13

The Brain Seeks Faith

Has it never occurred to you that perhaps your brain doesn't work quite as well as everybody else's? Are there never times when you suspect that maybe you don't have as much gray matter as other people do?

If not, good for you. Most of us are not so sure. When I was in junior high school I began asking myself questions about my own mental powers, and the fear that I might not be entirely all there bothered me seriously for some time.

Perhaps because of a subconscious memory of that experience, many years later—in fact, only ten years or so ago—I asked the great brain pathologist Professor Toshihiko Tokizane whether many people were actually born wanting in brains. Professor Tokizane, I'm sorry to say, has since died, but at the time he was not only a teacher at the University of Tokyo and head of the Institute of Brain Research there but also director of the Primates Research Institute, at Kyoto University. I had the good fortune to meet this great scholar on many occasions.

To my question, he gave a succinct answer: "Our creator distributed nothing so equally among human beings as he distributed brain matter. The question is how to use and develop it.''

We have this great authority's word for it, then, that we all have equal brain power. Why, we must therefore ask, does the brain work so well for some people and not so well for others? I should like to discuss this question here as it relates to the study of Buddhist truth.

Earlier I pointed out that if we had no brain, we would see nothing, hear nothing, feel nothing. For all practical purposes, our world exists inside our brain and therefore is a part of us. What we call our heart, the seat of our emotions and passions, is also located within our brain. Let us consequently consider the physical structure of the brain, as explained by Professor Tokizane, and see how it relates to the question that concerns us.

Below is a rough, but serviceable, illustration showing the main functional parts of the brain. At the center is the brain stem (medulla oblongata), connected to the spinal cord. Extending down over this is the cerebrum, which is the part we think of when we speak of gray matter. Back of the brain stem is the cerebellum.

Each of the three parts has a distinct sphere of activity in normal circumstances. The cerebellum mainly controls functions related to physical action or exercise. It is with this part of the

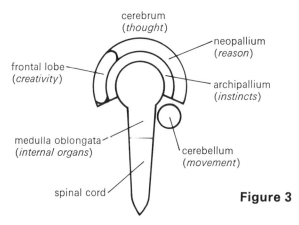

Figure 3

brain that we keep balance when we walk or run or jump or stand on our heads or swing from a steel bar. If it is injured, we tend to fall down.

The brain stem controls the body's internal organs. When you exert yourself strenuously, your heart begins to beat harder. This is because the brain stem has commanded the heart to increase your blood supply to correspond with the energy you are using. The brain stem also issues the orders that make our stomach work to digest the food we eat. It keeps our body temperature constant despite changes in the temperature outside us and maintains a constant sugar content in the blood flowing through us. Whether we ourselves are asleep or awake, this part of the brain works without rest, twenty-four hours a day, day in, day out.

The cerebrum is the part of the brain that makes people people. It is, in short, what we call our mind, as well as our heart. Although it is the largest division of the brain, it is only 2.5 millimeters thick and has an average area of only 2,240 square centimeters. From this thin layer of wrinkled gray matter, with a smaller surface than a page in a newspaper, come all our conscious thoughts, all our tears, all our laughter, all our anger, all our joy, all our sadness, all our hope. Here is where we meditate, store our experiences, separate beautiful from ugly, judge what is good and bad, decide whether we are happy or not. Without the cerebrum, nothing that we see, hear, or feel would exist for us. Stating the case the other way, our entire universe is contained within this single organ. Even the Buddha resides here.

How much do brains weigh? The average for a mouse is 1.6 grams; for a guinea pig, 4.8 grams; for a rabbit, 9.3 grams; for a cat, 31 grams; for a dog, 65 grams; for a monkey, 88.5 grams; for a gorilla, 450 grams. For human adults, the average weight is 1,400 grams for men and 1,240 for women.

There are many people who believe that intelligence is proportional to the weight of the brain. If this were true, we would have to conclude that men are smarter than women. Professor Tokizane, however, did not believe that the weight of the brain is directly related to the degree of intelligence.

It is not possible, of course, to remove the brains of living people and weigh them, and the recorded weights for people who have died and left their brains to science reveal no fixed pattern. The brain of Katsura Tarō (1848–1913), three times prime minister of Japan in the early twentieth century, weighed 1,600 grams, while that of the celebrated novelist Natsume Sōseki (1867–1916), a contemporary of Katsura, weighed only 1,415 grams. As opposed to the late Yokoyama Taikan (1868–1958), a well-known painter whose brain was found to weigh 1,640 grams, Anatole France (1844–1924) had a brain weight of only 1,017 grams. The brain of the German chemist Robert Wilhelm Bunsen (1811–99) weighed no more than 1,295 grams, which is nearly as little as the average for women today.

As far as weight alone is concerned, man's brain is no match for that of the sperm whale (9,200 grams) or the elephant (4,000 grams), but no one considers either animal to be more intelligent than man. If the relative weight of the brain to that of the body is considered, both white mice and sparrows boast higher figures than man. Though it has been argued that brain power is proportionate to the number of wrinkles in the cerebrum, this too seems groundless. True, the brains of mice and rabbits have perfectly smooth surfaces, and those of monkeys have far fewer wrinkles than human brains. But porpoises have even more brain wrinkles than human beings.

If neither the weight of the brain nor the number of wrinkles in its outer surface governs intelligence, why is it that some people have better and quicker minds than others? There is, for example, a marked difference between children and adults.

Looking more closely at the cerebrum, we find that it has two principal parts. On the inner side is the archipallium, which human beings have in common with many animals. On the outside of this, in human beings only, there is a larger layer called the neopallium. All our spiritual activity comes from the combination of archipallium and neopallium, both of which prove, under a microscope, to be composed of extremely small cells, numbering about 14 billion in all. At present, the population of the earth is about 3.6 billion, which means that each of us has in his brain roughly four times as many cells as there are people now alive. The curious part about this is that the total of 14 billion appears to be the same whether the brain belongs to a learned man from a highly developed country or an indigene from an African jungle. Furthermore, newborn babies have the full quota of 14 billion—such is the fairness with which brain substance is distributed. From this, it is plain that whether we pride ourselves on having more brains than others or lament our relative lack of them, we are barking up the wrong tree.

As suggested by Professor Tokizane, the differences in mental ability that we actually observe come not from the size of the brain, but from the way in which it is trained and developed. Though human babies have 14 billion brain cells, the weight of their brains is only about 400 grams, or roughly a quarter that of an adult brain. Within six months, this weight doubles, and by the time the child is seven or eight, his brain weighs about 95 percent as much as an adult's. The growth in weight comes from the links that develop between brain cell and brain cell—what we might call the "wiring" of the brain. How the mind of a child develops is largely a question of how these connections are formed. In other words, it is a question of education and religion.

The offspring of horses, elephants, and many other animals can walk within a day of their birth, and after two or three days they are usually able to follow their mothers around. Human babies, however, cannot even stand up until they are a year or so old. The reason for this is a difference in ways of life. If a newborn wild animal were to require a half year or a year to develop the strength to move on its own, it would doubtless be attacked and killed in infancy by enemy species. To avoid this, it is kept in its mother's womb until it is able to fend for itself. Not being exposed to such dangers, the human baby can safely leave the mother's body at an early stage. It is actually born early so that its brain can undergo development not possible in the womb. In the case of horses and elephants, the "wiring" of the brain is already complete at the time of birth. Once the connections have been established, any attempt to revise them is doomed. In human babies, the links are still quite incomplete at birth, and the mode in which they are ultimately set up is a matter of education.

Training, then, is more important than lineage. Through education the mind can be made quick, or it can be made dull. As someone has said, man is an animal that cannot stand alone without education. And the work of continually improving the "wiring" within the brain is the function of religion.

If the brain is not properly nourished, we do not become people, for the brain is, as noted earlier, the source of our humanity. Our bodies are made in such a way as to give special treatment to the brain and thus aid it to develop and to work hard. The functions of the body are to the brain what faithful knights once were to feudal lords.

An example can be seen in the supply of blood furnished to the brain. The average human being weighs about 60 kilograms, of which 1.3 kilograms (average for both men and woman) is the weight of the brain. The brain thus accounts for only 2.2 percent of the total. Yet it receives nearly 20 percent of the blood circulating in the body. Whether we are asleep or up and around, our heart pumps no less than 45 liters of blood per hour to the brain. Just how much this is can be seen by observing that a regular-sized automobile running at full speed uses only about 10 liters of gasoline an hour (5 liters for a typical small car). In the case of children, whose brains account for about 6 percent of their weight, the blood supply to the brain is 40 percent of the total.

Within our bodies, the brain reigns supreme. If we have an accident and lose a dangerous amount of blood, our muscles and organs automatically react in such a way as to cause the blood vessels supplying them to contract. More blood is thus made available to protect the working of the brain. In return for all the consideration shown it by the rest of the body, the brain acts in various ways to keep us conscious and in good mental and physical order.

We have already seen that the cerebrum is divided into archipallium and neopallium. The archipallium controls mainly the instincts, of which we have three—hunger, the sex urge, and the herd instinct. Hunger exists for the purpose of maintaining life; the sex urge, for the purpose of preserving the species; and the herd instinct, for the purpose of keeping people together. When the instinctive desires are fulfilled, we feel gratified; when they are not, we are uncomfortable and inclined toward anger or fear.

The mechanism whereby the instincts operate is not especially complicated. To take hunger as an example, when our stomachs are empty, the composition of the blood changes; the brain stem, which senses this change, signals the archipallium, which then orders our whole body to go in search of food. If we rummage around in the kitchen and find something, well and good. If not, we gradually become more nervous and irritable. When we eventually eat our fill, the blood composition returns to normal, and the brain stem notifies the archipallium as before. Once the archipallium has ordered the body to stop eating, we are no longer interested in food, no matter what tempting delicacy might be placed before us.

The urge for sex is roughly the same. We seek a person of the opposite sex much as we seek food when hungry. If we find gratification, we are happy; if not, we are uncomfortable or angry. If two male animals are alone on an island with one female, they fight until one wins out and takes the female. The loser can only slink away and pine. But since sex is not a matter of life or death, animals do not fight to the death over it—at least not because of the workings of the archipallium alone.

The other instinct is the desire to be in a group or tribe. You probably think this urge is comparatively weak, but actual experiments reveal it to be amazingly powerful. People who believe themselves to be so well-disciplined and self-sufficient that they could stay alone indefinitely, provided they were given sufficient food, turn out to need company. Shut them in a room where they can neither see nor hear anyone else, and within a day or two they scream to be released. Kept in solitary confinement too long, a human being can very well suffer a trauma from which he will never fully recover.

Not only people, but the other creatures living on this planet, are made up in such a fashion that they cannot live in isolation from other beings. Before man had reason to fear enemies from without, his fear of being alone amounted almost to an obsession. No doubt the Buddha had this fact of life in mind when he taught that "nothing has an ego."

Animals have minds that are controlled by the archipallium, just as people do. What makes people's minds much more complicated and mysterious is the interaction between the archipallium and the neopallium. Monkeys and chimpanzees have the suggestion of a neopallium, but nothing to compare with that of human beings. In lower animals it is completely absent.

The neopallium controls our wisdom, our emotions, and our thoughts. To acquire knowledge, to make judgments, and to create are all functions of this part of the brain.

With the addition of the neopallium, man acquired a new dimension. He developed a mind that was not satisfied with mere fulfillment of the instincts, but also craved fulfillment of higher spiritual longings. One of Jesus Christ's best-known statements is "Man does not live by bread alone." This might be rendered into the language of brain pathology as follows: "Snakes or birds or cats, which have only an archipallium, are happy so long as their hunger, sex, and herd instincts are satisfied; man, however, has a neopallium, and because of it he does not experience genuine satisfaction merely from eating his fill of bread or having sex with a compatible partner of the opposite sex."

Within the neopallium, the top, rear, and side sections receive information from without and store it in memory banks. The front section, in the forehead, then draws on this memory, adds supplementary information, and forms new ideas. This is where thought and creation take place.

Because of the workings of the neopallium, we are able to make value judgments or to determine what is good or bad for our own purposes. The realm of the intellect and the spirit lives for us in this part of the brain. Animals, having only the archipallium, know only the present; for them the future and the past do not exist. The concept of time is ours because of the neopallium, as is the ability to see the relationship between events of the past and those of the present and future.

We can sum up the functions of the neopallium by saying that it gives birth to the consciousness we call self. Of all things, self is the most uniquely human, but its presence gives rise to serious problems. The brain activity that gives us self-starting minds, furnishes us with personalities, and establishes our selves is a truly marvelous creation. Yet like all other things it has both a bad and a good aspect. From the self that it gives us comes self-conceit, competitiveness, unbridled ambition, and eventually the urge to dominate. Feelings of this kind, unless controlled, can cause people to kill one another.

What happens when the herd instinct collides with the urge to kill for personal advancement? Here we have one of the basic inconsistencies that keep mankind and the world in turmoil: by instinct men cannot live *without* one another, but until now they have never learned completely how to live *with* one another. The mind of man is full of incompatible, illogical conflicts of this sort. That we are beset with problems at every level—home problems, business problems, national problems, world problems—is owing to the inconsistency of the movements that go on within our brains.

We regard the atomic and hydrogen bombs as terrifying weapons, yet it was the human brain that discovered atomic energy, and it was the human brain that decided to use it in warfare. The human brain, more than any man-made bomb, is the weapon we must fear, because it controls man and rules the world.

We regard education as something that will give a person not only a wealth of knowledge but also the judgment and creativity to use it. We expect education to foster noble sentiments and to create strong wills. Let us always keep in mind, however, that the same education can breed the mind of a murderer.

Such being the case, we attempt to make our world safe by enacting legal and moral rules. By promising among ourselves to abide by these rules, we create a society of mankind, but society works only insofar as we keep our promise. When, because of the inconsistencies and conflicts within our brains, we deny the rights of the people who are in this with us, we are bound to have trouble on our hands.

And that is why people of our time are worried and fretful; why our national legislature is troubled by endless fighting; why nations make and break treaties as the demands of the moment seem to dictate.

How can we overcome confusion and conflict?

That is the function of religion.

In his *Shōbō Genzō*, the Zen master Dōgen talked about "total motivation" (*zenki*), by which he meant the totality of sources causing things to appear. Fusen Nakagawa, a colleague of mine in the field of engineering, has in mind a similar concept when he says, "What we mean by complete realization of potential is a state in which all functions are perfectly balanced and the entire mechanism is working in the most effective manner possible."

People argue, with good reason, that the world was intended to exist in a state of harmony, and I myself firmly believe that we who live in this world would not have been born here unless we possessed within ourselves all the powers we need in order to stay alive here. I am also sure that if we employed to the full all the faculties with which we are born a completely harmonious world would come into being.

A rock lying by the road performs all the functions of a rock. Dogs bark and run around and otherwise carry out all the functions of dogs. Babies suck their mothers' breasts, cry in the middle of the night, and wet their diapers as often as possible, thus admirably fulfilling their responsibilities as babies. There is no inconsistency in any of this. But adult human beings seem unable to use everything with which their brains are equipped. Specifically, they don't make full use of the neopallium, and particularly its front section.

Within our brains, the archipallium is always throwing up strong signals of instinctive desires. The intelligence residing in the neopallium is exercising a restraining force on these instinctive urges. The archipallium says, "You're hungry—eat something right now.'' The neopallium replies, ''No, don't eat while you're walking home. Wait till you get there and are seated at the dinner table.''

Twenty-four hours a day this conflict between the forces of libertarianism and those of conservatism continues. If we follow the neopallium, we deny ourselves what we want and pretend that we don't really want it. Our smiling faces hide the tears inside. We are brave and admirable. But this is not using all the power within our brains.

The truth is that the source of all misfortune and unhappiness lies in the conflict between the archipallium and the neopallium. By instinct we crave money, but our conscience forbids us to do what is necessary to acquire it. Death is approaching, but we do not want to die. Behind every human sorrow lies a mental conflict of this sort.

As the battle within our heads continues, the cerebrum sends a steady stream of bad signals to the brain stem. Since the brain stem is in turn sending constant commands to the body's internal organs, eventually the stomach develops an ache, or the blood pressure rises, or we have nervous spasms. Too much stress not infrequently leads to stomach ulcers.

Today hospitals are overflowing with patients. Doctors and nurses everywhere have their hands more than full. One reason why there are so many sick people is that both the minds of individuals and the collective mind of society are in a state of disorder. We are, in short, demented, and the cause of our malady lies in the inability of the archipallium and the neopallium to find the perfect balance that makes it possible for all functions to proceed harmoniously.

What is needed to achieve balance and universal harmony is religion—the religious power that can convert delusion into harmonious functioning. Religion exists in the front section of our cerebrum; our inability to use it to the full is the inconsistency that lies at the root of the world's problems.

My own mother long suffered from gastroptosis caused by nervous disorders, but as soon as she came to understand the Law of the Buddha she recovered, immediately and completely.

To use the front section of the neopallium to the full is to listen as much as possible to the Buddha's teachings, to follow his Law diligently, to use one's mind creatively, and to try constantly to be of service to others and to the world. It is said that Zen Buddhists practice zazen (seated meditation) in order to give respite to the cerebrum—to achieve a truce, as it were, in the battle between the archipallium and the neopallium. The effect is to allow the brain stem to function normally and without hindrance, so that the whole body, including that part of the front section that was dormant, works effectively.

Our minds and our bodies are one. People today often know this, yet refuse to believe that the blind have been made to see and the lame to walk through religious enlightenment. Such miracles are termed "unscientific." But, in fact, from the standpoint of brain pathology, faith healings are possible.

Some people seem even to resent this fact. Religion, they argue, is a psychological form of lobotomy. (A lobotomy, or operation to sever nerve fibers in the front lobe of the brain, is an extreme measure for eliminating the tensions in the minds of the extremely psychotic; like heart transplants, it is opposed by many as a violation of the sanctity of human life.) It is true, of course, that religion has quieted violent spirits and helped to make warlike people more peaceful, but it has done so not by eliminating a portion of the brain's functions, but by bringing the whole brain into operation.

Snakes and dogs and frogs have no need for religion because they have no neopallium. It is enough for them to follow the dictates of their instincts. Human beings, however, must have religion, or else the continuous conflict between the archipallium and the neopallium prevents them from living together in harmony.

It is a mistake to dismiss religion as something that is "fine for people who want to practice it," but of no use to those who do not. Insofar as human beings are human, religion is a psychological necessity, the efficacy of which has ample scientific corroboration.

14

Practical Is Impractical

There are many people in this world whose forced exposure to mathematics during their school years still causes them to shudder at the mention of the word. Arithmetic, algebra, and calculus are for them associated with head-splitting conundrums and flunked examinations and sermons from disappointed or irate teachers.

These people will, I believe, be pleased to learn about a nineteenth-century mathematician named George Boole, whose approach to arithmetic was refreshingly simple. In the first grade, we all learned, as indisputable fact, that $1 + 1 = 2$, $2 + 2 = 4$, $4 + 3 = 7$, and so on. Well, Boole decided that all this involved too many figures, so he set up a new system of his own that had only two, 0 and 1. No 2, no 3, no 4—nothing but 0 and 1. Now by Boole's calculations, some things turned out just as you might expect:

$$0 + 0 = 0$$

and $0 + 1 = 1.$

150

But what happens to $1 + 1$? The answer can't be 2, because there *is* no 2. This didn't bother Boole at all. He solved the problem as follows:

$$1 + 1 = 1.$$

This might seem a little confusing to some of you, but keep in mind that mathematics is a game played by rules, called axioms, which cannot be disputed once they're decided upon. In Boole's new arithmetic, $1 + 1 = 1$ was not a theorem or computation, but an axiom: it is true by definition. Using this axiom and others like it as a foundation, it is possible to build a theoretically sound structure for a whole new type of mathematics.

It is not evident from what has been said whether Boole was a genius or a nut, but in any case anyone ought to be able to make a perfect score on a test in his brand of arithmetic.

You ask, what good is it? If you can't count more than one apple. . . . Many other people had similar doubts, and for more than a century Boole's arithmetic was a mathematical curiosity, interesting only to mathematicians. Engineers and business people wanted nothing to do with anything so impractical.

But in the past twenty or thirty years, computers have come into wide use, and Boole's arithmetic has all of a sudden become very important. The illustration below will help explain why.

The figures show three electric circuits. In Figure 4, there are a battery, an electric lamp, and a switch. If the switch is closed, electricity flows through the wire, and the lamp lights.

In the other two circuits, there are two switches instead of

Figure 4   **Figure 5**   **Figure 6**

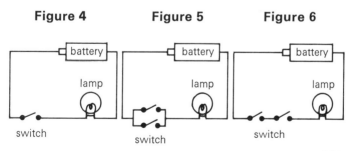

one. They are hooked up in parallel in Figure 5 whereas in Figure 6 they are in series. Let us call the case where the switch is open 0, and the case where the switch is closed 1. Similarly, an unlit lamp is 0 and a lit lamp is 1. Thus, if one of the switches in Figure 5 is closed, the lamp lights and we have:

$$1 + 0 = 1$$

$$\text{or} \quad 0 + 1 = 1.$$

But since closing both switches does not double the brightness of the lamp, we cannot say that $1 + 1 = 2$. Instead, we are left with $1 + 1 = 1$, which is Boole's axiom. Obviously, if neither switch is closed, the situation is $0 + 0 = 0$.

Moving on to Figure 6, we find something a little different. If either of the switches is open, the lamp does not light. Therefore, we have

$$1 \times 0 = 0$$

$$\text{and} \quad 0 \times 1 = 0.$$

If both the switches are closed, the equation is

$$1 \times 1 = 1,$$

since of course the closing of both switches does not affect the brightness of the lamp. Oppositely, when both switches are open we have

$$0 \times 0 = 0.$$

With a small number of simple circuits like this, there is no real need to drag in a weird system of figuring; a look at the diagrams is sufficient to tell what is going on. But when there are thousands or tens of thousands of switches, as in a computer, the diagrams are so complicated that they merely confuse. Traditional arithmetic, like $1 + 1 = 2$, is of no use either. The net effect is that more than a hundred years after Boole's death, $1 + 1 = 1$ has become a powerful mathematical tool.

The reason why I brought up the subject of Boole's arithmetic is that it has a bearing on a question that I am asked by nearly everybody who visits me at my laboratory. In this hideaway, deep within the university where I teach, there are all sorts of funny little mechanical devices: a monkeylike gadget, hanging from a cord, that is able to move backward or forward hand over hand; a thing that looks like a turret but has two legs with which it can jump forward like a frog; a box that can move backwards, forwards, or sideways on feet that look like skis; any number of other miniature contraptions that look like refugees from a toy counter. Everybody looks at them curiously for a while, and then everybody invariably says, "Wonderful, but what are they for?"

This question bothers me no end, because I can't answer it. What I usually say is, "I don't really know, but maybe twenty or thirty years from now, when I am dead and gone, somebody will figure out some way to use them."

People who hear this seem to say to themselves, "Think of it—not a care in the world! Why didn't *I* become a university professor?" Or else they are of a suspicious nature and assume that I am keeping the uses secret until I have received a patent. I have observed that though people in general don't ask painters or writers or musicians whether their creations have practical value or not; if you're an engineer, you're expected to be engaged in study having immediate applications. Unfortunately for me, my interest lies in what we might call imaginative, or imaginary, engineering.

As I see it, people today worry all too much over whether things are practical or not. If they do something today, they want to see concrete results tomorrow; an investment made now is expected to pay off handsomely within a year. This kind of thinking can lead to the mentality of the out-and-out profiteer, who shuts his eyes to anything that does not yield quick revenues.

It appears that when we are near the end of an era our vision tends to contract. Everybody begins to see only that which is useful or profitable to himself right now, and nobody has a thought for what might happen to the world in another hundred or thousand years. People become narrow-minded, society becomes avaricious, and as a result the world goes into rapid decline.

In Buddhism this is known as the Decay of the Life Span, which is the last of Five Decays that take place when the world is on its way to ruin. The outstanding characteristic of the Fifth Decay is that people's lives grow shorter and they themselves become correspondingly more short-sighted. Great inventions or developments do not occur in this stage of history.

When you think about it, most of the useful things in the world have resulted, as Boole's arithmetic did, not from considerations of what is useful and what is not, but from a search for the truth for its own sake. Another excellent example from the field of mathematics is what are known as imaginary numbers.

All of you learned about squares and square roots before you got to high school, but let me refresh your memory. The square of a number is that number multiplied by itself; the square root of a number is the number that must be multiplied by itself to yield it. For instance, the square of 3 is 3 times 3, or 9. The square root of 9 is therefore 3. The square of 2 is 4, and 2 is the square root of 4. One squared is 1, which is its own square root.

What about -1? You cannot find a square root for it, because there is no real number positive or negative which when multiplied by itself does not give a positive figure. (Remember that two minuses multiplied by each other yield a plus.) The only way to find the square root of -1 is to make one up, and that is what mathematicians did centuries ago. The square root of -1 is defined as i (or j), which in contrast to real numbers like 1, 2, and 3 is called an imaginary number.

The number i is of very little use in keeping household accounts or figuring out how much you owe the bank. For most people, it is as useless as Boole's $1 + 1 = 1$. Yet it is a fact that hundreds of years after the imaginary i was conceived, it turned out to be immensely useful in the newly discovered field of electrical engineering, where it is employed in drawing up designs for motors and transformers.

It's the same in many other fields. Many, if not most, of the great paintings, books, and musical compositions regarded as part of our cultural heritage were at the time of their creation scoffed at as the frothings of madmen.

Students today hear the famous statement ''I think, therefore I am'' and regard it as hyperserious to the point of absurdity. Who cares *why* I am, they ask—the point is that memorizing abstract philosophical statements like that is never going to make anybody a single cent. I see this attitude around me all the time. The young people do not see that the seemingly idle development of mental discipline can eventually enable a person to perceive truths hidden at the inner core of mankind and society.

Several years ago I went to Australia on my summer vacation and met with a delightful jolt. If you will recall, I mentioned among the playthings in my laboratory a box with feet like skis. I had made this for no particular reason—just thought it might come in handy some day—and now in Australia I saw, at an open-strip coal mine, the same device magnified several hundred times and carrying out Herculean functions. The skis enabled it to advance into the enormous, uneven coal field. Resting on them was the dormitory in which the miners slept, no less, and extending out in front was a gigantic power shovel, capable of lifting several large trucks at once. A look at this walking colossus set me to thinking once again how often something seemingly without rhyme or reason—something that would probably be described scornfully in Japanese as a ''long, useless object''—turns out eventually to be a boon to industry or society or both. I thought, too, how easily an insistence on now-this-minute practicality can give rise to waste and thereby sap our collective strength. That which appears to be meaningful and realistic turns out to be an illusion, while that which appears visionary and unrealistic turns out to be of prime significance.

Perhaps you remember the equation I introduced in a different context:

$$X = X'$$

where X' is anything opposite to X. We can fill in the unknowns here as follows:

real = unreal

practical = impractical.

The Australian machine led me to this result, but the moment it crossed my mind, I knew I had seen it somewhere else. But where? After a time, I finally remembered a place in the sixteenth chapter of the Lotus Sutra, the one on the life span of the Buddha, where Shakyamuni Buddha says, "The Tathāgata [i.e., Buddha] knows and sees the character of the triple world as it really is: to him there is . . . neither reality nor unreality. . . ."

If I am correct, this means that it is a mistake to assume that something exists just because it has a visible form; and that it is also a mistake to assume that something does *not* exist because it lacks a visible form. By extension, it is wrong to decide either that something has value because it is useful, or that it lacks value because it is not useful.

As I see it, this teaching of the Buddha does not mean that we ought to take care of apparently useless things because someday they may turn out to be useful. (That may not be a bad idea, but I don't believe it is the correct interpretation of the Buddha's statement.) The real meaning, I think, is that if human beings allow only those things that seem useful to them to survive, the world will become so limited in scope that nothing will go right.

We are surrounded by things that are extremely convenient to us, but we have a baleful tendency, arising ultimately from ego, to use them injudiciously. Without doubt one of the most convenient of all inventions is the automobile, in which we can travel long distances rapidly without having to worry about looking up train or bus schedules, or buying tickets, or having to kill time transferring, or arranging to get to and from stations. If you have a car and want to go somewhere, all you have to do is get in it and go. You can move into action on the spur of the moment; no planning is needed.

But we have discovered long since that the automobile is not a cause for untempered rejoicing. So many people attracted by the convenience of the machine have actually gone out and bought one that our roads are chronically clogged, particularly in cities. Traffic is such that cars can no longer carry people or cargo about quickly and freely over long or short distances. In other words, the original convenience has to a large extent ceased to exist. Or

convenience = inconvenience.

The original purpose having been lost, or at least obscured, people now buy expensive automobiles not because of their practicality, but because of their value as status symbols. Young people, unable really to get in cars and go where they want, work out their frustrations by removing their mufflers and speeding like roaring beasts down the streets in the middle of the night. The usefulness of the automobile has been overemphasized so greatly that it is now only apparent.

As I said before,

real = unreal.

And then there is the case of watches, certainly another of man's most convenient creations. A remarkable amount of technical skill goes into the making of watches, but a look at a sales catalogue will show you that people do not buy watches solely for their practical value. The catalogues carry everything from cheap vinyl-packed fad models that may or may not keep time to jewel-encrusted "chronometers" costing millions of yen. So far as accuracy is concerned, it appears that a watch selling for about ¥30,000 is just as reliable as models costing ten or twenty times as much, but it is no longer a question of mere practicality. Ornamental jewels and gold cases or bands have converted the wristwatch into an *accessory*. Carrying this trend a step forward (or is it backward?), designers have incorporated watches into necklaces, pendants, rings, and cigarette lighters. Do these decorative watches keep good time? Does it matter?

The clothes we wear have met with a similar fate. It used to be that we regarded wearing apparel as something to keep us warm in the winter and protect our skin from the sun's rays in the summer. Now, however, the purpose of clothing is to show other people what sort of a person one is, or would like to be. Aside from the perfectly absurd, in which the streets of our cities abound, there are even outfits that succeed in making the wearer look more naked than if actually naked. In clothing, we have reached the limits of unreality.

So although we are surrounded by convenient things, the world is also full of empty, impractical objects, most if not all of which began as something intended to meet a real need but got sidetracked somewhere along the way.

This is not to say that the Buddha condemned all empty, impractical things. He no more did that than he categorically praised all useful, realistic things. What the Buddha said was only that the things of this world are neither real nor unreal. But though I used the word "only," the truth is that to be able to view things in this fashion is to perceive and understand the cosmic force that binds everything together.

From a lecture on Dōgen's *Shōbō Genzō*, I made the following note: "We call pines pines and cryptomerias cryptomerias, but these are names that people have arbitrarily assigned to these trees. Nobody consulted the pine tree before naming it; nobody consulted the cryptomeria either. Have you ever heard a pine tree declare, 'I am a pine'? Or a cryptomeria tree declare, 'I am a cryptomeria'?"

We see the world from the human standpoint, but the pine tree also has its standpoint, as does the mountain peak, as does the ocean. The world is made up of all these standpoints. The Buddha's teaching is that we as human beings must not be obsessed with our own view of what is real and what is not, or else we shall miss the truth.

There is every likelihood that so long as we remain occupied with our own ideas of reality, we will not be able to see anything as it actually is.

Let me offer you an example. If we plant a chestnut seed, after a time it grows into a tree that flowers and bears fruit. Since we like to eat the chestnuts, we usually consider that at this point the tree has fulfilled its purpose—come to fruition, as we sometimes put it. For us, the fruit is the end result, the reason why we have gone to the trouble of planting the seed and cultivating the tree in the first place.

But from the tree's standpoint, the aim in putting forth fruit is not to feed human beings; it is to create a new generation of trees and ensure the continuation of the species. To the tree, the idea that producing the fruit is the goal and everything else up to that point a preparatory stage must be unwelcome, to say the least. In nature everything is part of a continually changing process; no phase can rightly be singled out as a preparatory stage or a final result.

We tend to forget that this rule also applies to human beings, who are as much a part of nature as trees. Generally speaking we fall into the fallacy of regarding childhood as a preparation for adulthood. That is where our troubles begin. Or at least it is where our children's troubles begin.

In this day and age, by the time a child is in the fourth grade, Japanese parents are thinking, ''We've got to get him into a good junior high school. If we don't, we won't be able to get him into a good high school, and then he won't be able to get into a good college. And if he doesn't get through a good college, none of the best companies will hire him.'' This when the child is barely ten years old! The child, as a result, is pushed mercilessly and without respite—forced to stay on his toes at all times. Symptomatic of this unnatural situation is the frightening phenomenon known as the ''education mama,'' who with the best of misguided intentions will sacrifice anything to see her baby through the best schools. All too frequently, that which is sacrificed is the child himself, for the system might as well have been deliberately designed to yield a maximum of nervous breakdowns and personality disorders.

Most Japanese children—boys in particular—go along with the system as best they can, believing, I suppose, that once they have finished college and found a good job, life will be a bed of roses. In present-day Japan, however, when they do reach this level, they discover that their first ten or fifteen years of work are merely a ''preparation'' for being promoted to the position of a section chief, which status is ''preparatory'' to becoming a department head and then, if they have not already reached retirement age and dropped out, a senior executive or president of the company. How many Japanese men, too far along in years to backtrack, discover that they have spent their whole lives in a state of "preparation" and there is nothing further to prepare for but death!

There is a Buddhist saying that "each and every day is a good day." Today is important not because it leads to tomorrow but because it is today. Every instant is to be lived to the full for its own sake. This does not mean that it is stupid or futile to have goals and be willing to sacrifice to achieve them. The point is that life is a cumulative series of moments and days, each of which must be lived to the full if life itself is to be lived to the full.

As the Buddha said, a total view of this world shows that there is no beginning and no end. A child is born, and while everyone is taking on over how cute he is, he is suddenly in school studying for exams, then marrying, then having children—and everybody is taking on over how cute *they* are. Then *they* are grown and married and having children and. . . .

It goes on and on. Just as the chestnut seed becomes a tree and grows and blossoms and yields chestnuts that fall to the ground and become seeds. Where is the beginning? Where is the end?

The reason why I am now absorbed in research that may or may not be of practical value after several tens or hundreds of years is that I want you to awake to your existence as part of a never-ending life cycle that is neither real nor unreal. Whether you perceive this or not will depend on whether you have a flexible or an inflexible spirit.

A flexible spirit begins when, in our associations with people, we learn to accept good-heartedly and open-heartedly everything that is said to us. When someone tells us something, flexibility requires that we think about it from all angles possible to us. We must ask, "What is this person teaching me? Is he showing me *this,* or is he showing me *that?*" If you look at things this way, the real meaning of what is being said will presently come to you in a flash. Everything will be clear.

Truth may be defined as natural law that pervades the universe.

The Buddha is preaching the Law—the truth—at all places and all times, but he does not force it upon us. Unlike the "education mama," he doesn't stand over us and command us to understand or memorize our lessons. If we do not actively seek in our hearts to hear him, he does not speak to us. A flexible spirit is indispensable if we are to understand the truth of his silence.

The opposite of a flexible spirit is an unyielding spirit—the egotistical attitude that causes us to ignore or misinterpret what other people say and to insist on having our own way. The inflexible spirit does not seek to hear. Most often, as a matter of actual experience, it must suffer a severe shock before it awakens to the truth.

But if the civilization in which we live cannot find enlightenment without undergoing a severe shock, we are in trouble, for the shock, whether it comes from pollution or war, might in this case be fatal. This is why I urge you to cultivate flexible spirits in yourselves, which you can best do by living a religious life. This is what the world needs today, and the need is urgent.

Explanatory Note

The Five Decays (Japanese, *gojoku;* Sanskrit, *pañca kaṣāyāḥ*) are five classes of evils that tend to prevail as the world approaches an end. They are as follows:

1. The Decay of the Age occurs when an era has grown long and old. It is characterized by war, natural disasters, pestilence, and famine. This might be described as the *fin de siècle* phenomenon.

2. Decay through Delusion is marked by hedonism and decadence. It occurs when people have no control over their baser instincts.

3. Decay through Egocentricism is a state in which society has become excessively complex, and people work only for their own selfish ends, neglecting the rights and needs of others.

4. Decay of Views results from the spread of heretical or evil ideologies, such as the idea that man is but an economic animal, or that history is entirely materialistic.

5. Decay of the Life Span is marked by the shortening of people's individual lives and by their resulting tendency to become shortsighted and utilitarian in attitude.

It requires no great insight to notice all of these defilements thriving in our twentieth-century world. The only way for us to banish them is to discover and practice the eternal Law of the Buddha.

15

The Virtues of
Negative Feedback

I have for some time been learning the truths of Buddhism one by one from the robots I make. It's like taking lessons from a child you've brought up.

People say, "Aside from whether you actually can learn from a robot or not, why do you want to study Buddhism? What use can it be to a scientist designing robots?" The idea seems to be that a scientist dealing with facts and proof has no business studying anything so unscientific as religion. A large following still clings to the notion that religion and science are mutually exclusive. I, on the other hand, am thoroughly convinced that religion and science exist for the purpose of arriving at one and the same truth. In fact, I am writing this book to prove the point.

The nucleus of Shakyamuni's teachings and of Buddhism is that all things are both related to one another and in a state of perpetual change. If I wanted to, I could express the same idea as follows: all things are in a state of eternally circulating change. My reason for rephrasing in this way is that I would like to emphasize the concept of circulation, which is a central factor in the study of cybernetics.

163

Cybernetics is a new science. It came into existence, in Japan as well as in Europe and America, after the Second World War, or about 1950. In the following decade, scholars in this field were regarded by other scientists as being circulation specialists, and in fact circulation was what most of us were studying. Our particular interest was in the circulation of information.

What purpose is to be accomplished by delving deeply into the question of how information circulates or is circulated? The purpose, I am happy to say, is to make a fundamental wish that all people share come true. And what might this wish be? What is it that we all desire every day of our lives? Is it not to have things go the way we would like them to go? How blissful we would be if they did!

At work you think, "Why doesn't this project go right? Why are there so many snags? And when will the company ever pay me enough to finance a little house of my own?" Life is full of questions like this: "Isn't there some wonderful girl (or boy) somewhere who wants to marry me?" Or "Will I really be able to get into the college I want to go to?"

In other words, every day we think, time and again, "If only things will go right. . . ." The effort, the ardor, that we put into our lives begins and ends with the yearning to make things go right.

But do they? Hardly. The rule seems to be that everything goes wrong if it possibly can. The role that specialists in cybernetics have cut out for themselves is that of making it possible for us to control things better.

Everyone knows how James Watt observed the steam coming from a boiling teakettle and resolved to use this energy to turn the wheels of a train. But have you ever stopped to consider the difficulties Watt faced? If you throw a lot of coal on the fire heating your boiler, the wheels attached to the boiler will begin to turn very rapidly. Alarmed, you may reduce the supply of coal, but you will find that the wheels do not slow down immediately. After a while, however, they not only slow down, but come to a complete halt. In order to make the wheels work right, you must create a device that will keep them at the same speed whether the pressure of the steam is high or low. You must, in other words, find a way to control the movement. The object of cybernetics is to invent controls that make things move as desired, rather than haphazardly. This involves much research into mechanisms for ensuring the proper flow or circulation of information.

To ride an unruly horse, we use reins, which we pull tight or relax as the need arises. The reins are our control mechanism, which depends for its effectiveness on the information we feed into it with our hands.

The word control, which epitomizes the aim of cybernetics, was frequently used by the Buddha. In the Dhammapada, for example, we find, "A person who can control his anger as he would stop a moving vehicle, I call a manager." And "To do no evil by thought, word, or deed—he who can control these three is called a saint."

To this I will add my own opinion: The sciences I am studying, cybernetics and robot engineering, deal with the problem of making machines move in the desired fashion; Buddhism, as taught by Shakyamuni, deals with the problem of allowing us to live, and our society to progress, in the desired fashion. Unfortunately, the society of man does not often operate as we would like it to. Present-day society in particular seems to have reached a complete impasse.

How can this be put right? Let us try to answer by applying methods of cybernetics to the Buddha's teachings concerning control.

Let us start with the principle that information circulates. Fundamentally, there are two types of circulation. In the first there is a cause coinciding with a specific condition to produce an effect, which itself becomes a new cause producing a new effect, which in turn becomes a second new cause and so on. The movement being ever forward, this is known as feedforward.

In the second type, there is again a cause combining with a condition to produce an effect, but instead of moving forward, this effect operates on the original cause, which now yields a new effect, which again operates on the original cause, and so on.

Since the effect acts upon the cause that produced it, this type of circulation is called feedback.

That the buildings we work and study in are kept at a steady temperature in the winter, warm enough for us to be comfortable, but not too warm, is the result of a feedback mechanism. Let us consider, for example, the case of students in a lecture room listening to a teacher. The room is heated by radiators, through which flows steam from a boiler. The warmth of the room increases when the flow of steam is made greater and decreases when the flow is reduced. The flow is kept at the proper level by a janitor, who controls it by opening or closing a valve. The janitor uses a thermometer as his guide.

Suppose it's a cold day with no sun and with the thermometer registering below zero. The janitor opens the valve wide. But if it's a balmy spring day, threatening to be too warm, he opens the valve only a little, if at all.

The temperature outside is the cause. The condition is what the janitor does to the valve after consulting the thermometer. The resulting rise or fall in the temperature of the lecture room is the effect.

But in actual practice the method outlined would not keep the room at a constant temperature. If word should get around that the lecture was to be a good one and sixty or seventy students crowded in to hear it, their body heat would raise the temperature inside higher and higher. Then, no doubt, someone would complain of the heat, and all the windows would go up, causing the room to cool very rapidly. The poor janitor could work up a sweat trying to adjust the valve to suit the students, but he would not be able to keep ahead of their complaints.

One hopes that after a time he would have a brainstorm and hang the thermometer inside the lecture hall, rather than out in the cold. This would give him a much better chance of pleasing the people inside.

Say the janitor wants to keep the temperature at 20° Centigrade but observes that it is only 17° in the lecture hall. The 3° difference becomes a cause moving him to open the valve. The effect is that steam flows through the radiators. The flow of the steam in turn becomes a cause having the effect of raising the temperature to 20°. If nothing further is done at this point, the temperature in the room will continue to rise, going up perhaps to 22° or 23° before the janitor notices it. When he does take heed, the reading on the thermometer becomes a cause resulting in his partly closing the valve. The effect is that the flow of steam is reduced and the thermometer reading falls. When it goes below 20°, it again becomes a cause for opening the valve. And so on and so forth, around and around. The back-and-forth effect constitutes feedback, because the effect is reflected onto the cause.

It remains to be observed that there are two kinds of feedback, positive and negative. Positive feedback is what would happen if the arrangement were such that a rise in the room temperature caused the valve to open wider. Negative feedback occurs when a rise in the room temperature is reflected back in such a way as to cause the valve to close and reduce the temperature. The janitor opening the valve when the temperature is low and closing it when the temperature is high is thus engaged in negative feedback.

It is, of course, possible to achieve negative feedback without the janitor's contribution. This is done by fitting the heating equipment with a thermostat, which is a simple type of robot illustrating a primitive form of cybernetics.

Today there are robots that can not only stand alone but also avoid falling over when they are temporarily thrown off balance. They are able to do this because they have a built-in negative feedback mechanism. If one of these robots starts to fall over forward, a signal (information) goes to the feedback device causing it to push the robot backward to counteract the fall. If the robot starts to fall backward, the opposite occurs.

It may be said that installing a negative feedback in a robot endows it with the power to reflect, and with this power the robot is able to stand or walk alone.

As I watch people and societies and nations in action, I am tempted to believe that everything that goes wrong does so because of positive feedback.

Not long ago I was on a jam-packed commuter train. For some reason, the train stopped suddenly, and everybody fell forward.

"Ouch!" shouted a student. "If you're going to trample on people's feet, the least you can do is apologize." With a violent shove, he pushed the offender away.

The latter, a man in work clothes, growled, "I didn't mean to step on you, you ass. I couldn't help it if I got pushed into you, could I?" To emphasize his point, he punched the student in the chest.

Student: "Yah, you wanna make something out of it?" Hook to worker's right jaw; straight jab to his left jaw.

By this time the train had pulled into a station, and as the door opened the belligerents tumbled out, beating and kicking at each other.

That is positive feedback for you. One blow leads to two; two blows lead to four. Anger increases geometrically on both sides, and the only possible result is a duel to the finish.

Take another example. You decide that you would like to have some money—100,000 yen, to be exact. You work hard and save diligently, and presently you have 100,000 yen. But then you discover that this makes you want 200,000 yen. Then, when you have 200,000 yen, you begin thinking that 400,000 yen would be better. And so on indefinitely.

It has not been too many years since the Japanese economy went through a period of wild inflation, brought on largely by the oil crisis of 1973. Panic buying was triggered by shortages of necessaries, like heating fuel and toilet paper. The truth was that the shortages were largely artificial—manufacturers and dealers had ample inventories, but were holding back on the expectation of higher prices. As a result, higher prices came, causing the manufacturers and dealers to become even more reluctant to part with their goods.

Labor unions proceeded to scream for higher wages. Employers cried out in turn for higher prices to offset the increase in labor costs. For a while wages and prices spiraled upward in a spectacular display of positive feedback. When a reaction set in, it came in the form of the worst depression in twenty-five years.

Positive feedback is escalation feedback—an explosive rise leading ultimately to a disastrous fall. This is the type of feedback that brings on what we all *don't* want.

What is to be done? The solution is simple in principle: switch from positive feedback to negative feedback. How? The answer offered by cybernetics is that somewhere in the vicious circle a minus value must be introduced.

In the case of our lecture room, we observed that positive feedback, in which a temperature rise caused the valve to open wider, would make the temperature rise indefinitely. This is because both the rise and the wider opening of the valve are plus values. If we fix it so that a rise in the temperature, which is plus, leads to the closing of the valve, which is minus, overheating can be avoided.

During the economic crisis I spoke of, heat begot heat until there was a danger that the whole structure would melt and fall apart. Fortunately, not long before it would have been too late, wiser minds prevailed in the government and certain parts of the economic world, and negative values were introduced. As noted, a depression followed, and it was a bad one, though not as bad as it might have been if inflation had continued on unhalted for a longer period. After the drop, a second negative feedback set in, this one canceling out the negative values of depression, and recovery ensued.

Thanks to a second oil crisis, we now find ourselves faced once again with runaway inflation. Let us hope that this time there will be manufacturers and dealers who hold back on price increases despite rises in the cost of materials and labor; laborers who will content themselves with moderate raises; housewives who will refrain from hoarding and refuse to buy products they do not really need. If, amid all the economic plus signs, there are a few brave souls who will bear the onus of introducing minus values, chaos can be avoided, at least to the extent of putting a stop to escalation. The next step, which is even more important, is to actually switch to negative feedback. This is not easy, but there exists a way.

If someone assaults you, you're apt to get angry and want to strike back. But if you can control your instinct and not retaliate, you can prevent positive feedback from setting in. The next thing to do is give your assailant a friendly pat on the back. If you can manage this, negative feedback will set in.

"You have heard that it was said, 'An eye for an eye and a tooth for a tooth.' But I say to you, Do not resist one who is evil. But if any one strikes you on the right cheek, turn to him the other also; and if any one would . . . take your coat, let him have your cloak as well. . . ."

These are the words of Jesus Christ, but they are also the instructions for negative feedback—as well as the teaching that one must follow to achieve the Buddhist essence of wisdom.

The Sutra of Innumerable Meanings says: "This sutra . . . makes a merciless one raise the mind of mercy, makes a homicidal one raise the mind of great compassion, makes a jealous one raise the mind of joy, makes an attached one raise the mind of detachment, makes a miserly one raise the mind of donation, makes an arrogant one raise the mind of keeping the commandments, makes an irascible one raise the mind of perseverance, makes an indolent one raise the mind of assiduity, makes a distracted one raise the mind of meditation. . . ."

If I were to rephrase this, I could put it very simply in the language of cybernetics: "This sutra tells you how to switch from positive to negative feedback, and thereby become good instead of evil."

The Buddha said, "To aspire to the Buddha-mind is to want to save others before saving yourself." This means it is not right to think, "Once I'm saved, I'll try to save other people," or "I'll save other people so that I myself will be saved." The first step is for you yourself to accept the negative role in setting up negative feedback. To be able to do this is to aspire to the enlightenment of the Buddha. Once you have the genuine aspiration, the result of the negative feedback you initiate feeds back in such a way as to save you.

The reason why this works this way lies in the basic principle that "nothing has an ego." In the interrelationship between this idea and the "aspiration toward the enlightenment of the Buddha'' and the principle of negative feedback, I see a beautiful example of the essential oneness of religion and science.

The question is, who will start the negative feedback? An answer can be seen in the following statement by Nikkyō Niwano, president of Risshō Kōsei-kai, a Japanese Buddhist lay organization: "Buddhism teaches that you cannot be happy without at first becoming a fool. This is something that those of us who have had the good fortune to encounter the Buddha's teachings must demonstrate to the rest of the world." The first step in becoming a fool is not to return violence for violence. If someone strikes you, just stand there and take it. That is the way to prevent positive feedback. The second step is to do the opposite of what was done to you—smile and bow to the person who attacked you. No one can do this without becoming a first-class fool by normal standards. Yet the fool who has the courage to start the negative feedback process is possessed of the wisdom that can turn evil into good. Clever people who see only to the ends of their noses cannot follow this path, but for the brave it is the true way to peace and happiness. If you take a look around, you will see that those things which are functioning smoothly and harmoniously are doing so by means of negative feedback.

This is true, for example, of our bodies, whose negative feedback systems keep our blood pressure, as well as the sugar content of our blood, at a constant level. If something upsets the feedback mechanism, we get sick. Were it not for the negative feedback that makes us feel satiated after we have consumed a certain amount of food, we might well eat until we damaged our stomachs. Compulsive eaters, unable to stop when they are full, suffer from chronic physical disorders. Basically, they are victims of a type of positive feedback.

One form of negative feedback is to make up for differences between yourself and the person you are dealing with. The trick is to keep your eye on him and do whatever is necessary to keep pace with him. It's like the two wheels of a cart, which must compensate for any variation in each other's speed if the cart is to go straight.

The first requisite is to size things up accurately. Once you know what is going on, you can begin considering ways to stop positive feedback and set up negative feedback in its place. The action you devise is invariably reflected back upon you. If you save your fellow men, you yourself will be saved. Keep in mind that even robots are now acquiring the power to reflect, and that the theory making it possible to control robots is but another proof of the theory underlying the Buddha's way of saving us. Science and religion, far from being opposed to each other, are in this respect identical with each other.

A Buddhist priest I know has said, "We must completely destroy the idea of a conflict between religion and science. Einstein said, 'Religion without science is blind. Science without religion is deformed.'"

It is my firm belief that by remembering this and by working together in good faith we can save our world from the crisis of contemporary civilization.

16

The Buddha-nature
in the Robot

A young man recently confronted me with this question: "Just where is the buddha-nature in us located? Is it in our heads, or in our hearts, or somewhere else?"

The buddha-nature is one of the first things a person thinks seriously about when he begins to study Buddhism. I felt sure that the youth talking to me had recently developed an interest in Buddhist thought. Nor was I wrong.

He continued, "Buddhism teaches that everyone has a buddha-nature that he must cultivate and perfect through the practice of religion. One way of doing this, I read, is to pay respect to the buddha-nature in others. But I don't understand just what part of me I ought to cultivate, or which part of another person I ought to pay respect to. The more I think about it, the less I understand."

"Yes, I see," I replied, meaning that I saw his problem, not that I saw the answer. The question is one that the matter-of-fact young people of our time are apt to be troubled by, but I was not sure I could explain the buddha-nature in terms the young man

173

would understand. In fact, I began wondering if I myself really understood where and how it exists within us.

Perhaps you would say, "Don't be silly. Anybody knows the buddha-nature is in our minds and our emotions."

I thought about that, but it's not enough. The Buddha said that "all things" have the buddha-nature, and "all things" clearly means not only all living beings, but the rocks, the trees, the rivers, the mountains as well. There is buddha-nature in dogs and in bears, in insects and in bacteria. There must also be buddha-nature in the machines and robots that my colleagues and I make.

Having said this, I hasten to confess that I didn't remember ever having put anything called a buddha-nature into a robot. If the young man had asked me what part of the robot it inhabits, I would once again have been at a loss for an answer.

Since the young man's question continued to bother me, I resolved to do a little research. Having looked through a number of books, I remembered that Dōgen's *Shōbō Genzō* has a section on the buddha-nature. The gist of this writing, as translated freely by myself from a lecture given by Yuian Iwasawa, is as follows: "When we say that everyone has the buddha-nature, it sounds rather as though the buddha-nature is an organ like the heart or liver, but this is not the case. The buddha-nature has no physical form and is not confined to one part of the body. It fills the whole and all the parts. The hands, the feet, every single hair contains the buddha-nature. Furthermore, the buddha-nature is present in the earth and in that which grows upon it. It is present in the wind and in the sea. It inhabits that which feels and that which does not feel; it is present in delusion as in enlightenment. Everything that exists is made of the buddha-nature. This body of ours was created as a manifestation of it, and the purpose of our religious activities is to recover it in its original state."

The buddha-nature, then, is the principle or law that moves everything. It exists throughout the universe and fills it completely. It is impossible for us to get outside the buddha-nature. We are like the monkey in the famous Chinese novel, who traveled to the end of the world and back only to discover that he had never left the Buddha's hand. The buddha-nature takes us back to an idea I mentioned before: it is neither real nor unreal.

Earlier I wrote in some detail about the folly of seeing only that which has form and not seeing that which lacks it, or of treasuring that which is important to yourself while demeaning that which is not. If we are to see the real truth, we must open our eyes wide and break through the confines of man's egocentrism. We must see that excrement and carrion, the odor of which makes us want to hold our noses, may make a splendid feast for a hyena or a vulture or a fly. The carbon dioxide we exhale as waste is a necessity for plants, just as the oxygen that plants give off is a necessity for us. Everything that exists in this world has a meaning. It is beyond presumption for human beings to decide merely on the basis of their own needs or their own likes and dislikes what is valuable and what is not. The first point in locating the buddha-nature is to quit valuing only that which we find convenient and denigrating that which we do not find convenient.

Unless we adopt a broader sense of values, we will not be able to see that the buddha-nature is present in all things. Instead, we will find it in people who are good to us, but not in those who treat us badly. We will be able to detect the buddha-nature in a good, faithful watchdog or a playful, tail-wagging dachshund, but condemn a dog that snaps at us as a useless cur.

In most recent summers, the water in Lake Okutama, which is Tokyo's main source of supply, has fallen to dangerously low levels. Not long ago, when a typhoon brought heavy rainfall to the Okutama district, everyone breathed a sigh of relief—until the water overflowed and the current swept away houses downstream.

The water that keeps us alive and the water that crushes life is the same water, but it is not easy for us to see that its buddha-nature is the same in both cases. Shakyamuni Buddha set an example for us in cases like this. With respect to his cousin Devadatta, who attempted to kill him, he said, "I must recognize his buddha-nature, for he is the benefactor who led me to enlightenment."

The point of departure for learning to see the buddha-nature in everything is the realization that all things are neither real nor unreal. When we see the relationship between real and unreal in all phenomena, we will have no difficulty with the idea that everything is created by the buddha-nature.

The earth and the sun will serve as an example. If I were to tell you that the sun moves around the earth, you would protest that to propound the geocentric theory at this late date is unscientific in the extreme. But from another star, the earth and the sun must appear to be rotating around each other, like linked stars. If the sun is considered to be in a fixed position, then the world appears to move around it; but if the earth's position is considered to be fixed, then it is the sun that appears to be rotating. The main point of the theory that Copernicus and Galileo staked their lives on was not that the earth is revolving around the sun, but that the sun, the moon, and the earth are all celestial bodies floating in space.

It is the same with the land and sea on our planet. When we are not thinking very hard, we consider the land, on which we live, to be completely separate from the sea, where the fishes and the octopuses live. On the other hand, we customarily regard lakes as belonging to the land masses. If asked how lakes differ from the ocean, we explain that lakes are surrounded by land, whereas the ocean is not. But take a look at a world globe. To the Buddha, whose view of the earth is like ours of the globe, it would appear that the land is surrounded by ocean and that the ocean in turn is surrounded by land. The truth is that the land is the land because the ocean is the ocean, and vice versa. The one gives the other its identity.

We are now in a better position to attack the problem of the robot's buddha-nature, but for a moment let us consider the machine that we call an automobile, which is considerably simpler than a robot.

I'm sure most of you have a driver's license. You consequently know that when you want a car to go to the right you turn the steering wheel to the right and when you want it to go left you turn the wheel to the left. When you want to stop, you step on the brake, and so on. This is all a simple matter of control, and everybody considers it perfectly natural. The steering wheel and the brake are devices for letting the automobile know what you want it to do, just as the bit and reins are means of letting a horse know what you want it to do. And since you impose your will on the car (or the horse), you have the powerful feeling that you are causing it to behave exactly as you wish.

But one day when I was driving my car to work, an unsettling thought occurred to me. Why am I so sure that it is I driving the car, rather than the car driving me? In order to make the car move in a particular way, my hands and feet must also move in a particular way. In a sense, the car makes them do that to get it to do as desired. The more I considered the actual motions I went through to control the machine, the more it seemed to me that I was more driven than driving.

The situation is like the one we observed in trying to distinguish between land areas and sea areas. Depending on how you look at it, I could be regarded as managing the automobile, or it could be regarded as managing me. To control, in effect, is to be controlled: by driving the car properly I enable it to play a safe and useful role in life; but by controlling me, the automobile enables me to be a reliable and effective driver. The same relationship links human beings with all machines. They don't do what you want them to do unless you do what they force you to do.

There may be those who object to this line of reasoning. It could be argued, for example, that if the car were more completely automated, it might not be necessary for us to use our hands and feet to make it carry out our will. Could we then say that the automobile was controlling us?

The answer of course is yes. Think for a moment of those automatic doors that open when you step on a mat in front of them. One can easily imagine a device that would not require our stepping on the mat—or even walking in front of a photoelectric cell. There might perhaps be an audioelectronic attachment that would make the door respond to the words "Open sesame," as in the *Arabian Nights*. In fact, if money were no object, I see no scientific reason why we could not make a door that would open or shut when we just *think* "open" or "shut." The most advanced artificial arm and hand now made can in fact pick up a cigarette from a table when the wearer simply wills it to do that. A specially designed electrode is attached to the muscles of the wearer at the point of contact between his body and the artificial limb, and an increase in the flow of electroneural energy in the muscle caused by the wearer's *wishing* to pick up the cigarette activates a motor that causes the arm and fingers to carry out the action.

No matter how highly automated a mechanical device may be, however, it remains necessary for us at least to *think* the command that activates it. We could therefore say that the machine exercises control over our very minds.

Anyone who has trouble in accepting the reciprocality of the relationship between men and machines may observe the same principle in operation between machine and machine, where mentality is not involved. An example that comes readily to mind is that of a thermostat used to regulate the temperature in an artificially heated room. When the temperature goes below a certain predetermined point, the thermostat turns the heat on; when the temperature has risen to the desired degree, it cuts it off. The thermostat, if it had a brain, would doubtless consider itself to be masterminding the climate in the room. On the other hand, if the room could talk, it would probably claim that it was in control of the thermostat, which automatically responds to the room temperature.

Since we draw a mental and verbal distinction between the thermostat and the heating system and the air in the room, we are inclined to try to decide which controls which. But in fact the three are functioning as an integrated unit.

All right, you say, but it remains a fact that when men and machines are involved, men have wills and machines do not. Is it not an insult to the dignity of man to suggest that machines are not subordinate to him? This question, it seems to me, makes it necessary to ask just what human will is.

I can produce a robot in such a way that when its batteries are about to give out it will automatically seek a source of electricity—a socket or other outlet—and get them recharged. I can, in other words, endow the robot with a hunger instinct and the ability to satisfy it. To all appearances, when this robot begins to run out of power, it moves of its own free will to an electric socket that can revitalize it. Yet in truth I, the designer, give the robot its appetite; it is I who cause it to act as it acts.

The robot's relationship to me is like my relationship to the Buddha. I, like all other human beings, was created by the Buddha (by the Void). Every movement of my hands or feet, every blink of my eyelids, is the result of the Buddha's will. There is no way in which a human being's body or mind can separate itself even momentarily from the Buddha's laws. To express it differently, men are appearances brought into being by the Void. This is what Yuian Iwasawa meant when he said that "every single hair contains the buddha-nature."

How is it with machines? Reason dictates that they too must be "appearances brought into being by the Void." Some may argue that this is not true: that machines are made by men. But if men are appearances created by the Void, then whatever men create must also be created by the Void. It must also partake of the buddha-nature, as do the rocks and trees around us. Specifically, since I myself was created by the Buddha, the machines and robots that I design must also be created by the Buddha.

In sum, a human being made by the Buddha and endowed by the Buddha with a will necessarily imposes that will upon a machine created by the Buddha. The truth is that everything in the universe is identical with the mind of the Buddha. That which controls and that which is controlled are both manifestations of the buddha-nature. We must not consider that we ourselves are operating machines. What is happening is that the buddha-nature is operating the buddha-nature.

From the Buddha's viewpoint, there is no master-slave relationship between human beings and machines. The two are fused together in an interlocking entity. Man achieves dignity not by subjugating his mechanical inventions, but by recognizing in machines and robots the same buddha-nature that pervades his own inner self. When he does that, he acquires the ability to design good machines and to operate them for good and proper purposes. In this way harmony between human beings and machines is achieved.

How can this principle be applied to everyday human relationships?

Let us imagine a young businessman jostling his way home on a crowded commuter train during the evening rush hour. The office is still very much with him. "What a grind!" he thinks. "The boss was pretty happy with himself today, but how would he feel if he had to do all the dirty work? How would he like driving himself to the breaking point every day of the world for the paltry salary I get?"

To the much-put-upon average employee, the man sitting at a desk all the time ordering other people around appears to have it very soft. All he has to do is open his mouth and people jump to do his bidding. He doesn't spend his time bowing and saying "Yes, sir—just as you say, sir."

But this view fails to take into consideration the mental strain of being a manager or executive. No one who has never had a staff of people working under him can know just how difficult it is to get other people to do what is desired of them. The baseball manager sits in the dugout and barks out orders. Without moving, he can change pitchers, or send in a pinch hitter, or order the batter to bunt. On the surface he is the great man exercising power, doing nothing himself, just basking in the glory of a commanding general. But think of the responsibility he accepts. If he miscalculates, he loses the game and is held accountable for the loss. And it is not as though he himself were in a position to pitch a shutout or drive in the winning run.

Many is the business executive who at times wishes he could take the time to do a job himself rather than depend on a subordinate. To manage people effectively, the executive must constantly consider how each of his subordinates feels about his job, how he will react to a given order, how he can be used in such a way as to conserve the executive's own time and effort. The executive's work begins with the fact that he is surrounded by people different from himself, who do not always perform as he wishes them to.

When we speak of executives and subordinates, we imply a superior-inferior relationship, but this is only apparent. In reality, executive and subordinate can function only in a single organization in which the executive is as much used by his helpers as they are by him.

I once served on a panel of judges for an idea contest. There were about sixty entries, and we spent an entire day going through them one by one. Afterward, one of the ideas that we had thrown out kept coming back to me; I couldn't escape the suspicion that we had acted too hastily in eliminating it. When I asked the people in charge of the contest what had happened to this entry, I found that it had in fact proved to be a great practical success.

To myself I thought ruefully that to judge is also to be judged. I had been evaluated by a splendid contest entry and had been found completely incompetent.

The above thoughts, inspired largely by my robots, gave me an answer to the question that we must all confront sooner or later, which is to say the basic question of how we ought to lead our lives.

That which human beings most desire in this world is genuine salvation. How can we achieve it? The solution is simple in the extreme: to be saved, we must save. All we need do is forget about saving ourselves and direct our attention to saving others. If we do this thoroughly, earnestly, selflessly, there will come a day when we ourselves are saved. Buddha-nature will evoke buddha-nature: that is the great principle that governs the workings of all nature.

I succeeded in finding out from robots the most important rule of all for living. Human beings, who have minds, are constantly being thrown off the track by complications. The picture is rarely clear. We are told that everything has the buddha-nature, and we try to act accordingly. But then we discover that someone we know has done something perfectly execrable, and we begin to doubt. "How," we ask ourselves, "could anybody who would do an evil thing like that have the Buddha inside him?" We feel that our trust has been betrayed, and we resent the person even more than if we had never expected any better from him.

But robots are simpler than people. So are mountains and rivers and plants and animals and insects. If these less complicated creatures begin to cause us difficulty, we have no trouble seeing that the fundamental cause is our own failure to function in accordance with the principles of the universe. The machines, the mountains, the rivers, the plants, the animals, the insects all tell us that we, who are filled from head to toe with the buddha-nature, have nevertheless not succeeded in being what we ought to be.

When we forget to pay proper respect to the buddha-nature in the wind and the water, typhoons and floods inform us of our lapse and show us in no uncertain terms how we have not lived up to the buddha-nature within ourselves. When we forget the buddha-nature in automobiles and other machines we have created, a warning comes to us in the form of accidents or pollution. What everything in the universe is constantly saying to us is that the way to perfect our own buddha-nature is to respect the buddha-nature in other things and other people.

17

Accepting the Incomprehensible on Faith

Several years ago I remember going down to Yokosuka one day on some personal business. Halfway back, just after my train pulled out of Kawasaki, we came to a sudden stop and didn't move for quite some time.

After four or five minutes, the conductor came on the loudspeaker and said, ''Reports are that 800 student activists have invaded Shimbashi Station, up ahead of us, and fighting has broken out among them. We ask your patience for the time being.''

''Good heavens!'' I thought, ''800 of them, lambasting each other with staves and pipes!''

''What are we going to do with those kids?'' sighed a woman near me. ''Why do they always have to be killing each other?''

It was hot, and the passengers were visibly irritated. After an hour the train finally started up again, and fifteen minutes later we were passing through the aftermath of the carnage. So many rocks had been thrown that the platform at Shimbashi resembled a gravel road. The whole place was littered with helmets, and the police had gathered a small mountain of sticks and bamboo poles. Bloodstained headbands and T-shirts were scattered in profusion.

"What makes them do it?" was the thought that haunted me. It was better back in the days when they hated the universities and the professors. Now they were lashing out even more virulently at each other—at their own flesh and blood, as it were. Student violence, now more than ten years old, had already claimed a fearsome number of dead and wounded. Obviously it was still escalating.

Once they had all been comrades. Why was it that now one look at each other drove them to fratricide? Cooler heads had urged them to lay down their makeshift (though potentially lethal) weapons and fight on the ideological level. To which they had scoffed, "Trust those pigs? Don't be crazy! There's nothing to do but stamp them out completely."

As I stood in the train thinking about this reaction, I remembered something I had read: "He who has faith but no comprehension increases in ignorance. He who has comprehension but no faith increases in evil views." This is from the Sutra of the Great Decease, and the recollection of it at that moment was spine-tingling.

The members of the Zengakuren, the nationwide Marxist student organization from which the now-warring factions all descended, were suffering from a surfeit of comprehension without faith. By comprehension, I mean the ability to analyze—the intellectual capacity to differentiate and discern, down to the finest differences. Endowed with superior intelligence, these students had understanding of a sort, but, lacking faith, they had all too palpably "increased in evil views." Because of this, they were able now to do nothing but doubt, and their doubts had given rise to murderous rivalries and enmities among them. Why had they forgotten how to believe and learned only how to doubt? Could it not be that we, their teachers, and particularly those of us who taught them the natural sciences, were largely responsible for making them this way?

When you think of it, the natural sciences, which scholars study and expound to students, begin with the spirit of doubt. It was not enough for Newton to know that God made the apple fall from the tree; he wanted to know if there were not some other reason comprehensible to men. The scientist starts with a suspicious attitude. When experiment justifies his suspicion, he accepts it as proven truth. Something that has been proved can no longer be doubted. It is, by its very nature, scientific fact.

The scientific approach is extremely important. It is the scientist's duty to doubt, to experiment, and to try to arrive at indisputable proofs. If we are not careful, however, the scientific attitude can lead to a dangerous result, which is a tendency to reject that which science has not proved. It is one thing to believe wholeheartedly in that which has been explained scientifically, but quite another to refuse to believe that which science has not been able to explain.

Indeed, the very essence of faith is to believe in that which has not been explained and may never be explained. To have faith is to say to yourself, "I haven't proved this—I don't know exactly what it consists of or how it works or what result it will lead to—but I believe it." Faith is not needed to accept what has been proved intellectually. It is what we know intuitively to be true that must be accepted on faith. By the very act of believing, we acknowledge that what we believe may be genuine or false, right or wrong, truth or fiction, but that we are determined to believe it anyway.

Admittedly, there is a danger in this attitude, too. To hold stubbornly to a creed when there is no intellectual support is to run the risk of "growing in ignorance." Yet unless we have the courage to put doubts behind us and believe in certain things that have not been and may never be proved, we cannot get along in the world we live in. It just won't hold together.

Consider this, for the moment, on the personal level. Suppose you have a friend who has a reputation for being a liar. People will say, "If you believe what that character says, you'll lose your shirt."

What do you do? Do you say to yourself, "All right, until he's proved himself to be honest, I'll be careful"? That would be the normal reaction, but it wouldn't help to remedy the situation at all. Your being suspicious is not going to make an honest person of your friend or anybody else.

But suppose you say, "Okay, maybe there's a certain amount of danger, but I like him and I'm going to trust him." You would be surprised at the effect. There is every chance that your friend will be honest with you whether he lies to other people or not. It is very difficult for most people to betray someone who they know trusts them. This is the power of faith: it brings out the good in people. To put it another way, you can evoke the buddha-nature in another person by paying reverence to it.

If we all trusted each other, wouldn't this be a wonderful world to live in? Mutual confidence would be a great pipeline serving to bring us all together and prevent us from injuring one another. We could help each other and thereby find greater happiness for ourselves and others.

We do not come into the world doubting. In early childhood everybody has absolute confidence in his parents. Unfortunately, when children begin to grow up, sooner or later they have the experience of being betrayed—not once but many times. Inevitably they go through a phase in which they are convinced that nobody is to be believed. "I'll never trust anybody again as long as I live" are words that everybody has uttered at one time or another. There's nothing exceptional about it.

Human beings are not perfect. Whether on purpose, or of necessity, or unwittingly, we all betray other people from time to time. It is hardly surprising that by the time young people are grown many of them consider it the mark of wisdom to be skeptical. This attitude may indeed be prevalent among adults today.

But is it really foolish or childish to trust people? Is it clever always to be in doubt? If one takes a narrow view and thinks only of immediate gains and losses, perhaps it is. But I look at it differently. If you are conferring with someone or making a request of him, the whole drift of the conversation is governed by whether that person trusts you or not. People sense other people's feelings and change what they say to suit the circumstances. Doubt cannot really be concealed. And doubt gives rise to distrust, which creates resistance and may lead to out-and-out conflict. This is the reason for a great deal of the unhappiness that all of us suffer as we go through life.

We need to stop and think. It is impossible for one person to be happy all the time and everybody else miserable. By the same token it is impossible for everybody else to be happy all the time and one person—you alone—miserable. The only way for a human being to be truly happy is for him to be happy together with others. In the very short run, it may be folly to place one's trust in people, but the greater wisdom enjoins us to believe. This is the meaning of the Japanese saying that "the sage resembles the fool." The trust we need more of today is the lofty mutual trust of mature people building a happy human environment together. How can we create that trust? The key is to live in accordance with the principles of the universe—to live in such a way as to bring out the buddha-nature that resides in all things and all beings.

Some of the confusion and difficulty we experience in the world today seems to me to arise from a mistaken view of democracy. Many people appear to have the notion that democracy means equality for all in every respect; they are not happy unless men are the same as women, students the same as teachers, parents the same as children. On the face of it, this is ridiculous—men can't have babies; students can't teach school; children can't provide for parents; nobody wants to give the vote to infants. Yet our failure to work out standards that would be fair to all leaves everybody with the suspicion that he is being imposed upon—that he is not as equal as he ought to be.

Not long ago I dropped a small bomb at my house. I have three children in school, and as a rule I am the last to leave in the morning, but on this particular day I had to be at the university early. As I was going out, I waited for a moment at the front door, but nobody came to see me off. My children were all watching television.

Outraged at this breach of Japanese etiquette, I shouted, "Hey, what kind of a dump is this? Doesn't anybody believe in giving the breadwinner around here a sendoff?"

"Just a moment!" came the reply as all three of them scrambled out to the front hall. "Goodbye, Daddy, have a nice day." It would all have been very touching if I hadn't had to ask for it. What, I wondered, is the world coming to?

But when I sounded off about this to one of the younger professors, he merely sighed and said, "I envy you, sir. At least your children do what they're supposed to do after you remind them. When I tell mine they ought to do this or that, they don't say, 'Yes, father.' They say, 'Yeah, I know.' But then they don't do what I told them to. If they *know*, the way they say, then that must mean they're deliberately paying no attention to me. But then nobody seems to expect children to listen to their parents any more. We live in evil times."

If you ask a young person why he ignores his parents, he will answer something like this: "Oh, what they say is so old-fashioned you'd think they were a hundred years old. It just doesn't make sense in this day and age. How can we be expected to understand a lot of old-fogy ideas?"

The words might be different, but the gist would be that young people can't understand why their parents think as they do. This, I believe, brings us back to what I was saying before: this is the reaction of young people brought up in an age of doubt, an age of science. But the truth is that nobody can really understand what someone else is saying unless he has a similar degree of experience, knowledge, and judgment. For children not to understand their parents is nothing brought on by the spread of scientific knowledge. What we owe to science is the notion that children need not learn what they don't understand.

In order to understand a parent, you must *be* a parent, just as you must be fifty years old to understand people that age. Once you are fifty *and* a parent, you are in a position to understand what your mother and father were saying forty years ago, but by that time it's too late.

As human beings, we will not really be able to understand the teachings of Shakyamuni until we have arrived at the same sphere of enlightenment as he. But to do that we must die and be reborn in the cycle of reincarnation hundreds and thousands of times. If we pay no attention to the Buddha until after we've done that, it will be too late. That is why we have faith: it enables us to believe without fully understanding.

Our parents and our ancestors are to us as guides who have preceded us along the way. Unless we recognize their authority and respect them, there is no way of transmitting or preserving the culture to which we belong. This remains true in the most democratic of ages.

The young may counter that parents make mistakes too. Was it not, after all, their parents' generation that started the Second World War?

This argument is not without reason. If the young believe everything they are told, they stand to be deceived in the worst way. There is never even any guarantee that one's own father is right. How to overcome this drawback is one of life's great difficulties. Still, if there is an atmosphere of mutual trust, even mistakes and blunders can furnish food for thought, which might lead to the discovery of new values.

To trust one's parents or one's elders is not, after all, to swallow everything they say whole. In this respect, we can derive a lesson or two from some of the many anecdotes that are told concerning the eccentric Zen priest Ikkyū (1394–1481).

It is said that when Ikkyū was five, he was sent to a temple called the Ankoku-ji as an acolyte. As he grew, he proved himself to have a great deal of native intelligence and wit.

He was one of seven acolytes at the temple. One day when they were all talking together, one of them remarked on how the temple priest had taken to staying up late at night. "There's something funny going on," he commented. "Nobody likes to sleep better than he, but the past few nights he's been sitting up by the lamp till all hours."

The next night, after everybody else had gone to bed, Ikkyū stealthily took up watch outside the priest's room. After a time, the priest went to the closet and from its depths removed a jar of rock candy. Plopping a piece into his mouth, he sat for a time sucking contentedly.

Ikkyū knocked on the door and entered. Feigning surprise, he said, "Why, Master, whatever is in that jar? It looks just like rock candy." Whereupon the priest gulped down the sweet in his mouth, tucked the jar into the folds of his robe, and replied with an air of shocked innocence, "Candy, child? What could you be thinking? This is medicine. At my age, the cold makes my legs and back ache so that I have to take something to relieve the pain. This is a palsy remedy. It's so strong that one taste of it would kill a boy your age."

"Oh, I see," replied Ikkyū sweetly. "It's medicine for you, but poison for children. In that case, I suppose I'd better not ask you to give me a piece. Good night, Master, sleep well."

After the boy left, the priest smiled to himself. "Never doubted it for a moment," he thought. But a surprise was in store for him. The next morning, he went to the nearby village on a little business, and when he returned, all the acolytes were in his room weeping and wailing.

"What's going on?" he cried. "Why are you all here? What's all this weeping?"

Voice quaking with sobs, Ikkyū answered, "Please forgive us, Master. We were cleaning your room and one of us dropped that ink box of yours—the one you treasure more than life itself. It's broken beyond repair. We decided that we would have to commit suicide to atone for the loss, so we took all that medicine you said would poison children. We're waiting now for death to come." And Ikkyū fell to crying again.

The priest, caught in the act of eating his rock candy, had committed two sins: he had given in to his own selfishness, and he had lied. Ikkyū had outdone him by demonstrating two immutable truths: that all things are impermanent (the ink box) and that he who is born must die (the "suicide").

Deeds like this earned Ikkyū such a reputation for sagacity that the great shogun Ashikaga Yoshimitsu (1358–1408) expressed a desire to meet him. When Ikkyū, accompanied by the priest, arrived at the shogun's palace, Yoshimitsu said, "I heard that you are a very clever boy, and I thought perhaps you would do me a favor. See that screen painting there? Well, at night the tiger in it sneaks out into the town and attacks innocent people. This has caused a great deal of trouble, and I would like to get you to tie up the tiger for me."

Yoshimitsu could not suppress a grin as he made the absurd request. The priest and all the others thought the shogun had outwitted Ikkyū, but Ikkyū showed no signs of distress. He simply sat for a time staring thoughtfully at the painting.

At length he said, "All right, I'll do it. Please have someone bring me a rope."

The rope was brought and placed by Ikkyū's side. Taking one end in hand, he stood up, took a stance, and shouted, "Quick, now! Somebody chase the tiger out into the middle of the room. I'm waiting."

Instead of complaining to the shogun that what he was asking was unreasonable, Ikkyū accepted the challenge at face value and threw it right back. Yoshimitsu was forced to admit defeat, but he still had another trick up his sleeve.

Showing Ikkyū to a different room, he ordered the servants to place dinner before him. When the meal appeared, it consisted of a number of dishes that priests are forbidden to eat—a broiled sea bream, sashimi, and several other delicacies made from the flesh of living creatures. Yoshimitsu waited gleefully to see how Ikkyū would react.

But Ikkyū's only reaction was to dig right in and start eating with gusto.

"What's this, Ikkyū?" asked the shogun. "You're a priest, yet you're eating fish?"

Ikkyū swallowed what he was chewing, then replied nonchalantly, "It's only passing through—my stomach is a thoroughfare."

Genuine devotion to the Buddha consists not in fasting but in seeing life within the flow of existence and in finding truth within change. All things are constantly moving and shifting. No matter what it is—money, possessions, knowledge, information—if you attempt to take it in and stop it from moving, you will be out of harmony with the universe. By following the natural flow of things, you can be guided by that greater harmony—such is the truth implicit in Ikkyū's statement about his stomach being only a thoroughfare.

Had Ikkyū allowed himself to become indignant or angry, as young people today might do when they think they're being taken lightly by their elders, he would not have been able to respond with such ingenuity. He would not, in fact, have perceived the truth concealed within the situations confronting him.

A passage in the *Muchū Mondō* (Conversations in a Dream) by the early fourteenth-century Zen Buddhist Musō Kokushi, says, "Teachers, being human, make mistakes, but that is no reason to deny everything they say or to forget how to learn from them." The same is true of parents.

In this volume, which might have been entitled *The Parable of the Robot,* I have tried to discuss various truths and principles of Buddhism in terms that make sense to young people living in a scientific age. I would be the first to agree that what I have written does not go beyond the limits of intellectual comprehension. It does not attempt to explain faith, which involves not only reasoning but also a deep personal conviction. The second-century Buddhist philosopher Nāgārjuna wrote, "In the great sea of the Buddha's Law, faith is the means of entry, and wisdom is the means of salvation." Today, we might say that science offers doubts and proofs, while faith makes it possible to live a good life.

If we only doubt and never believe, we injure others and eventually destroy ourselves. I firmly believe that if we are to realize the full potentialities that exist in this world, we must be able not only to doubt and prove but also to act courageously on faith when the occasion demands.